The Detroit and Cleveland Steam Navigation Company's New Steel Steamer, City of Cleveland,
Lake Erie Division   Season 1886.

CHIMNEY ROCK

A Lake
Tour
To

PICTURESQUE
MACKINAC

BY
C. O. WHITCOMB.
DETROIT MICH.
ILLUSTRATED
BY
SPECIAL ARTISTS

HISTORICAL
AND
DESCRIPTIVE

WM. GRAHAM & CO. DETROIT.

The Wood Engravings and Sketches

were executed by Van Leyen & Co., Detroit, Mich.

Entered according to Act of Congress, in the year 1887,
By. C.D. WHITCOMB,
In the office of the Librarian of Congress at Washington.

Reprinted by
Old Mackinac Press
P.O. Box 660
Mackinac Island, Michigan 49757
www.oldmackinacpress.com

ISBN: 978-0-9827221-2-1

ACATION is a cessation of work, and a diversion of the mind into new and pleasant channels. While it may seem like idleness to loll around at the seashore, the country farm or among the mountains, it is a repairing and oiling of the machinery, necessary to the better accomplishment of work. f you can find rest and recreation during the sultry months, you gain thereby. A water trip best quiets he nerves, rests the body and diverts the mind. We leave carping cares behind as soon as afloat, we cut loose and drift away from worries and anxieties of office, study, workshop and household, are interested in the changing scenes and in the enjoyment of solid comfort, float lazily and dream. We revel in the freedom, the dolce far niente, the pure, bracing air, the beauties of sky and sea, watch with fascination the leaping spray at the steamer's bow, fall to noting the ever-changing billows, and enter into projects for amusement started by others, or, originate them ourselves with the zest of a child.

On board a steamer we live a new, novel and fresh life, such as is never experienced on land. To those who enjoy great Nature's work, we would say:

Mackinac Island is among the grandest and most romantic of spots. Visitors are voluble with story and legend of every bold cliff and cave and fallen rock around the island, and many a pencil, brush and camera are brought to bear on the wonders found. Every section of the country sends visitors annually. The invalid is attracted by the wonderful purity of the atmosphere, the climate being noted as a sanitarium for hay fever and bronchial affections. Great numbers visit this region to escape from or get relief of these maladies; many experience an improvement on entering Lake Huron. No other resort possesses such entertaining features. The surrounding country offers endless attractions to the adventurous. Gamey fish lurk in all the inland lakes and rivers with which the State of Michigan abounds. Its forests are the hiding places of furred and feathered creatures, which afford fine sport.

Mackinac Island is reached by the Detroit and Cleveland Steam Navigation Company, by the pleasant lake route, with a splendid line of palatial iron steamers, the largest, swiftest and most luxurious on fresh water, forming the only comfortable route to this island resort. These floating palaces were recently built especially for the summer tourists' travel. The forward and after saloons, in mahogany and walnut respectively, are magnificently appointed and tastefully decorated, and their elegant rooms and parlors are replete with modern improvements. The lower saloons are devoted to dining halls, which entirely separate the culinary departments from the main saloons, a desirable feature only possible on these large side-wheel steamers. Their bill of fare, which is equal to that of any first-class hotel, includes all the luxuries of the season, and the price charged barely meets the outlay. Berths are in rooms, an upper, single width, and a lower, double width, in each, are furnished with wire and hair mattrasses and Pullman blankets. These steamers have water tight compartments, and their feathering paddles give unusual speed, without jar or noise. This water trip cannot be excelled anywhere, and the round trip affords a daylight view of all the route. No more comfortable place can be found outside of one's own home in which to spend the sultry days, than on board these splendidly appointed steamers. The changing scenes and fresh, bracing air, will benefit many who vainly seek relief at physicians' hands, and physicians urgently recommend this particular trip.

Bird's Eye View of Cleveland Harbor, as seen from the decks of Detroit and Cleveland Steam Navigation Company's Steamers.

CLEVELAND has a population of 210,000. Its distance from Detroit is one hundred and ten miles by water, and one hundred and seventy-two by rail. The city was founded in 1796 by Gen. Moses Cleaveland, and is one of the wealthiest and most prosperous cities of the west. Its manufacturing advantages, which attract capital from all parts of the country, are chiefly located in the valley, leaving much of the higher lands for residences, thus causing strangers to wonder where the business that is necessary to support so many inhabitants is carried on. The improvements of the city are worthy of special note. The breakwater constructed by the government is one mile long, and encloses two hundred acres of still water. The viaduct is an immense structure; length, 3211 feet, cost, $2,150,000. The N. Y. C. & St. L. R. R. viaduct, which is 3,500 feet long, is another monument of engineering skill. The business portion of the city is lighted by electricity, from the top of huge iron masts, ranging in height from 200 to 260 feet. It is called "Forest City," on account of its beautiful lawns and broad, shady avenues.

There are fine cemeteries and public and private parks. Lake View park is a famous promenade, and thousands visit it to delight in the cool breezes, and watch the beautiful sunsets, which are visible only where land and water hold a similar relation. Wade park, of one hundred acres, lies four miles from the city hall. Lake View cemetery is an extensive enclosure, combining the advantages of nature and art. It contains many grand monuments and costly tombs. Here lie the remains of the illustrious Garfield.

These steamers stop at the island both ways, giving those who wish to return on the same trip, from four to six hours in which to view the curiosities and wonders, or, you can return by one of them every thirty-six hours. Tickets for transportation can be procured from any ticket agent. Round trip tickets are good for the season. The round trip occupies four and one-half days from Cleveland, or two and three-quarters days from Detroit. The few landings made en route are just sufficient to interest without being tedious. Some of your neighbors have certainly made this trip. Enquire about it.

The Cost from Cleveland—This item has received our thoughtful consideration, and is the least possible to insure complete comfort, tickets covering transportation being only $5.00 one way, or $8.00 round trip; (half fare for children between five and twelve years of age.) Meals are 50 cents each; the same for children over three years old; under that age, 25 cents, and for the first table. The running time, Cleveland to Mackinac, includes five meals at 50 cents each, or $2.50 each way. Some passengers bring their own lunch. An upper berth of single width is $2.00, a lower berth of double width $3.00. Each room will accommodate three persons, by two occupying the lower berth. Put the items together, say for

	Single Trip	Round Trip.
Transportation....................................	$ 5 00	$ 8 00
5 meals at 50 cents each.........................	2 50	5 00
An upper berth for the trip.......................	2 00	4 00
Total with upper berth........................	$ 9 50	$17 00
Extra for a lower berth...........................	1 00	2 00
Total with lower berth........................	$10 50	$19 00
Two persons in one room ($9.50 and $10.50).......	20 00	36 00 or $18.00 each.
Three persons in one room add the.............		
transportation and meals only for the extra person	7 50	13 00
Total cost, Cleveland to Mackinac................		
for three persons occupying but one room.......	$27 50	$49 00 or $16.34 each.

o

Detroit Harbor—Showing Water Front of City and Character of Shipping

DETROIT, with a population of 150,000, is the oldest city of the west, and the commercial metropolis of Michigan. It is essentially a manufacturing city, and its peculiar advantages will eventually render it the Birmingham of the Northwest. It challenges comparison as being the handsomest city in the Union. In addition to its acquired beauties, it is extravagantly favored by Nature. The dwellings are mostly detached, with plenty of intervening space, the broad streets and prevalence of shade trees give the place a village air, and contribute much to its attractiveness for residences. As a healthful city it is without a peer. The beautiful river, ⅝ of a mile wide, affords the city a water front miles in extent, gives immediate escape from heat, dust and noise, and time need not hang heavy as there are a dozen popular, healthful and beautiful resorts within one to three hours' ride by steamer. There are eighteen islands, many of which are attractive for excursion parties and residences. Just above the city, Belle Isle park, containing 700 acres, is a favorite resort. Detroit is a complete and most desirable summer resort, combining all the requirements of a popular watering place, and the luxuries of a city home. The river is the pride of its residents, and the surprise and delight of tourists, who pronounce it the most beautiful stream in the world. Through it passes the vast tonnage of the lakes, which exceeds that of our foreign commerce. Our artist cleverly illustrates the character and activity of its shipping. Early settlers found on its shores homes more attractive than their wildest dreams had pictured.

This delightful trip by water, of 940 miles in the round trip, occupies 4½ days, costing only $16.00 to $18.00, or about $3.75 per day. You cannot go anywhere and compass so much enjoyment and solid comfort by the way. By rail you reach Mackinac a few hours earlier possibly, which is all that can be said in its favor, and is of the least consequence when seeking, pleasure, rest and recreation. It is certainly hot and dusty, you are cramped for room, and the little strength you start with is likely to be used up, especially is this the case with ladies and children. A summer trip should be planned to get all the quiet and fresh air possible. Why do you leave home at all? Simply to reverse the excitement of business cares, the bustle, hurry and rush. Such complete relief is only found by taking a water trip, the scenery is varied and attractive, and there is ample time for a good look at every interesting object. One way by steamer would be better than all rail. The outside expenses by rail will pay the cost by water. Have you taken this view of the matter?

Steamers City of Detroit and City of Cleveland, which form the Lake Erie Division with a nightly service (Sundays excepted) leave Cleveland at 8.30 o'clock, arrive at Detroit the following morning at 5.30 o'clock. Returning, leave Detroit at 10.00 o'clock, arrive Cleveland 5.30 o'clock, standard time. The fare between the two cities is $2.25 single trip, which is one-half of rail fare, or $4.00 round trip. Upper berths are $1.00, lower berths, $1.50. Among the advanced steps taken by this Company is that of not including the cost of berths in the ticket fare, which happily disposes of the vexatious question, how to best care for the comfort of our patrons. Commercial travelers, usually confined to the hot, dusty, noisy rail car, avail themselves of the charming quiet, cool, fresh air and the luxury of a full night's rest afforded by this night line by water.

Passengers can time it to make close connections at Detroit with steamers City of Mackinac and City of Alpena, which form the Lake Huron Division and leave every Wednesday and Friday mornings at 9 o'clock, Monday and Saturday nights at 10.00 o'clock for Mackinac and principal Lake Huron ports. The quickest trip and closest connection is made by taking Steamer City of Cleveland Tuesday or Thursday evening from Cleveland. Breakfast on board before changing steamers.

Bird's Eye View of U. S. Government Canal and the St. Clair Flats. The famous Fishing and Shooting Grounds. Home of the Black Bass and Duck.

1. St. Clair Hunting and Fishing Club. 2. Rushmere Club. 3. Butler's. 4. Star Island Hotel. 5. Boydell's. 6. Peninsular Shooting and Fishing Club. 7. Bedor's

8. Canadian Club House. 9. North Channel Club House.

MARINE CITY, 43 miles from Detroit, at the mouth of Belle river, has 2,000 inhabitants. No place of its size in the country has so extensively engaged in ship building. A bed of salt rock was recently discovered after boring to the depth of 1,700 feet, and a superior quality of the saline is now manufactured. The process of dissolving the rock is by pumping the St. Clair river water into the well, which washes the rock and becomes brine; it is then forced up into tanks and made back into salt. This great basin of salt, which as far as discovered is 115 feet thick, promises to make this the center of a great salt producing country. Those seeking rest from business cares would find this place both quiet and attractive, and unembarrassed by the strict social formalities so common to fashionable resorts. Hotel accommodations are comfortable, and rates reasonable. It has all the advantages of the much and justly praised St. Clair river, is but a short distance from the shooting and fishing grounds at the Flats, and has the best of facilities for obtaining information of the doings of the outside world.

The conspicuous enterprise of the Detroit and Cleveland Steam Navigation Company in furnishing palatial steamers, famous for comfort and speed, is fast bringing the happiest results to the banks of the beautiful St. Clair river. They have brought to notice the desirability of the site for summer cottages, and have left along the shores an incentive to improvement, which is fast making them bright 'with unnumbered shapes of new delight.'

The first steamer, constructed from two canoes spread apart, having a bow and stern fitted to them, was placed on this river some fifty years ago.

The Cost from Detroit—Transportation is $3.50 single, or $6.00 round trip. The running time includes four meals at 50 cents, or $2.00 each way. An upper berth of single width is $1.00, a lower berth of double width is $1.50 for the trip.

Put these items together, say for

	Single Trip	Round Trip.
Transportation	$ 3 50	$ 6 00
4 meals at 50 cents each	2 00	4 00
An upper berth for the trip	1 00	2 00
Total with upper berth	$ 6 50	$12 00
Extra for a lower berth	50	1 00
Total with lower berth	$ 7 00	$13 00
Two persons in one room ($6.50 and $7.00)	13 50	25 00 or 12.50 each.
Three persons in one room, add transportation and meals only for the extra person	5 50	10 00
Total cost, Detroit to Mackinac.		
for three persons occupying but one room	$19 00	$35 00 or 11 67 each.

A single individual desiring to occupy a room by himself, can arrange for it at an advance of the above prices. Meals and berths are arranged for exclusively by the company.

This delightful trip from Detroit to Mackinac by water, a distance of 740 miles in the round trip, occupying 2¾ days, costing only $11.50 to $12.50, or about $4.00 per day, is within the reach of a large number who make a practice of leaving home for a short time during the summer months.

It is not expensive by steamer.

These steamers being side-wheelers and large, afford the utmost comfort.

Parties who intend taking the Wednesday or Friday morning steamer, and arrive in Detroit Tuesday or Thursday evening, will be accommodated with rooms for those nights without extra charge, if applied for early in the evening at the General Passenger Office.

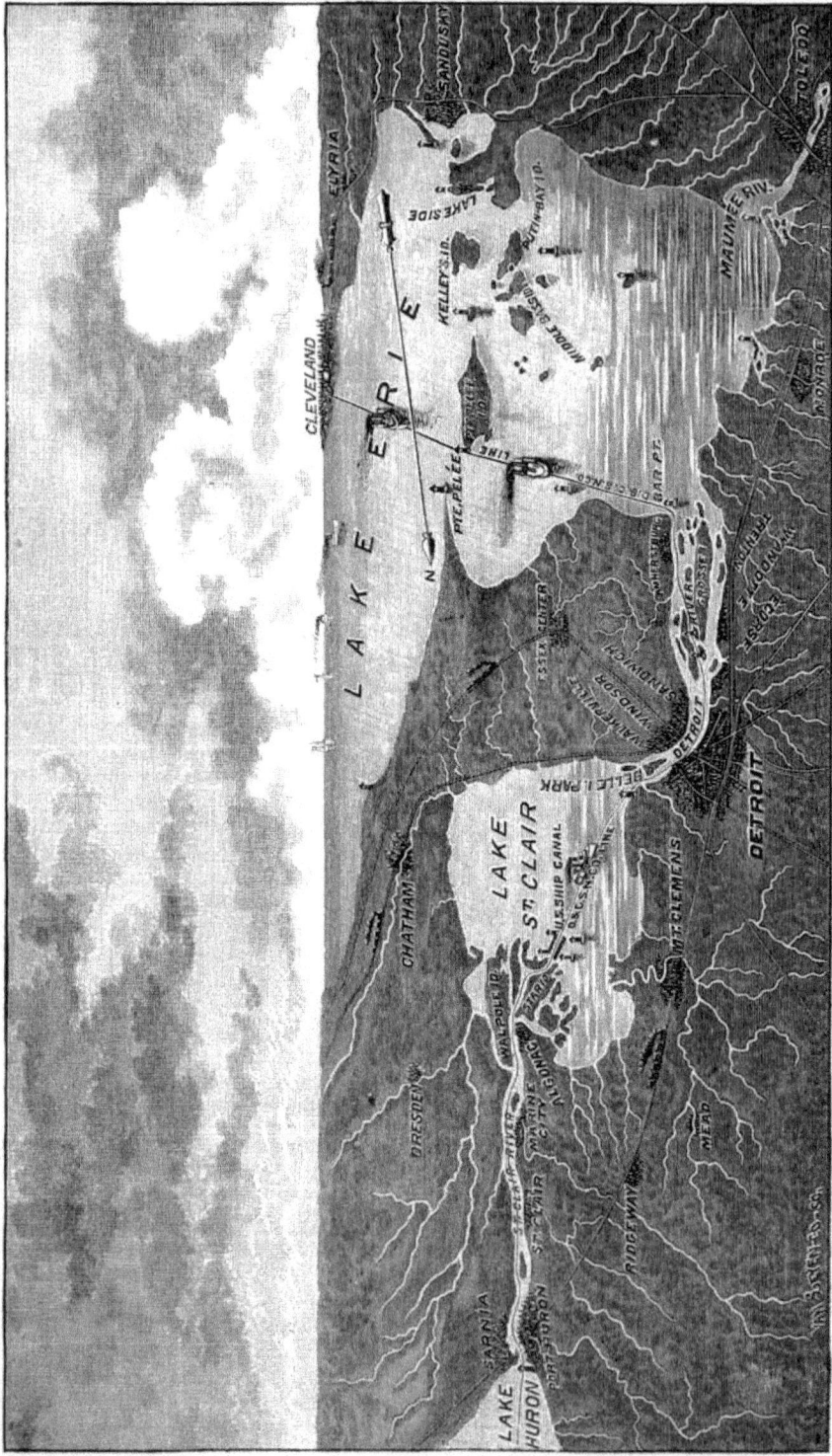

Bird's Eye View Lake Erie Division, Detroit and Cleveland Steam Navigation Company.

Easy of Access.
Beautifully Located.
Elegantly Appointed.
Moderate in Charges.

———————— ◉ ————————

THOSE who are looking forward the coming summer to spending the heated term at some resort, have, in selecting a place of sojourn, to consider where the most favorable combinations of climate, comfort, refinement and accessibility exist together, and in presenting the Oakland Hotel to the notice of the tourist, it is with confidence that it possesses in a pre-eminent degree the conditions mentioned.

Situated on the beautiful St. Clair River, connecting the chain of the Great Lakes, the summer temperature is always bracing and pleasant, and the nights delightfully cool. The steamers of Detroit & Cleveland Steam Navigation Co. stop at the Oakland en-route to or from Mackinac Island, while steamers from Detroit, Chicago, Duluth, Cleveland and Buffalo, stop frequently at its dock, and two trains from Detroit, Port Huron and Buffalo, respectively, afford direct connection with all parts of the country. The testimony of the thousands who in the past have visited the Oakland from all parts of the Union, and who speak in its praise, is the best guarantee that the Oakland, in its structure, arrangements, and general management, and in providing abundant first-class accommodations, has realized the designs of its projectors; while the persistent efforts to eliminate all that is objectionable, has rendered the Oakland pre-eminent in the refinement of its society.

The provisions for out and indoor amusement are most complete. Music and Dancing Hall, Shooting Gallery, Billiard Parlor, Boating, Lawn Tennis and Livery, each and all are of the best, while the Fishing is most excellent, and in immediate vicinity. The grounds are brilliantly lighted by electricity, rendering evening strolls and amusements a prominent feature of enjoyment. The Oakland has become renowned for entertaining large social clubs and organizations, and for which, with its facilities and location, it is perhaps unexcelled in the country. Special arrangements will be made with such parties on application.

But the inducements offered to the tourist, as above, are not all nor least, and what is perhaps the greatest attraction of all, is in its celebrated ST CLAIR MINERAL SPRING, and the bathing facilities of all descriptions provided in its superb Bathing Houses. To this Spring have come for restoration to health Vice-Presidents, Eminent Lawyers, Physicians, Financiers, Prominent Railroad Officials and Business Men, together with the Votaries of Fashion. No one has ever visited this Spring without being cured or greatly benefited.

Among the diseases this water is particularly adapted to, are RHEUMATISM, PARALYSIS, KIDNEY AND BLADDER DISEASES, NERVOUS AFFECTIONS AND FEMALE DISEASES.

The Spring is under the superintendence of a thoroughly educated and experienced Physician, who has for years made the water and its efficacy in curing disease his special study.

SUMMER RATES.
JUNE 15TH TO OCTOBER 1ST.
$17 50 TO $24 00 PER WEEK.
Children under twelve years, half price

WINTER RATES.
OCTOBER 1ST TO JUNE 15TH.
SPECIAL LOW RATES FOR THE WINTER WILL BE GIVEN BY WEEK OR MONTH, ON APPLICATION.

———————————

To those desiring fuller information, our illustrated pamphlet for 1887 will be mailed free, by addressing,

THE OAKLAND HOTEL,
ST. CLAIR SPRINGS, MICH.

THE OAKLAND HOTEL AND HYGIONAMA.

Open the Year Round.

ST. CLAIR, 50 miles from Detroit, has a population of 2,500. The location is a charming natural site at one of the widest and most picturesque points on the river where the shore makes a grand curve, giving the town, built upon its high and sloping bank, a most commanding appearance. The St Clair Mineral Spring is the great attraction. The waters of this spring, through the public spirited liberality of a few enterprising citizens, have become famous for their healing qualities. Connected with the spring is the Oakland Hotel, with a frontage of six hundred feet, with rooms unusually large and elegantly furnished, where guests will find every possible comfort and amusement provided, such as billiards, shooting gallery, bowling, swimming baths, and other in-door amusements, while on the lawns may be found the different games of the day. At the boat houses are clean, dry boats. The livery establishment supplies rigs of all descriptions, from the Shetland pony and cart to the stately landau, the spirited Kentucky saddler and spacious park wagon. For riding and driving a fine road extends along the river, a distance of thirty miles. There are numerous attractions in and about the Oakland, which will be best appreciated by a personal visit. A bath house adjoining the hotel has thirty handsomely furnished rooms.

There has been expended on the Oakland buildings and grounds a quarter of a million of dollars, not including an extensive tract of timber land, which is being developed into a pleasure park for the benefit of Oakland guests. The views from the hotel verandahs which face the river are grand. The changing moods of Nature and the floating commerce of man vary the delightful scenes, constantly adding new life and interest.

The Trip to Mackinac. The Steamer City of Cleveland or City of Detroit leaves the Company's wharf, 23 River street, Cleveland, at 8.30 p. m. Fifteen minutes are consumed in getting out of the river. A bright light on the port bow marks the crib built as a protection to the lake tunnel through which the city receives its water supply. From the end of the piers our steamer heads for Point Pelee Light, sometimes called the Dummy, which is fifty miles from Cleveland and sixty from Detroit. Point Pelee is a headland on the Canadian shore, projecting several miles into the lake at the entrance to Pigeon Bay, and with the many islands in the vicinity, form the most picturesque scenery on Lake Erie. We then head for Point Pelee Island Light. This island contains a few inhabitants, and abounds in red cedar and fine limestone. Several small islands lie to the south, called East, Middle and West Sister, Hen and Chicken, North, Middle and South Bass, Put-in-Bay. and Kelley's Island, the latter famous for its grape culture and native wines. From Point Pelee Island we run across Pigeon Bay to Colchester light ship, then to Bar Point light ship near the entrance to Detroit river. If you care to rise at this hour—about four—you will be well repaid by the early morning trip up the river. The river is twenty-seven miles long, and one-half to three miles wide, with a current of three miles per hour.

On the left, just before reaching Detroit, is Fort Wayne, which is garrisoned and mounted with heavy ordnance. We land at the Company's wharf, foot of Wayne street, at 5.30 o'clock in the morning, and passengers for the interior take their immediate departure. Passengers for Mackinac and Lake Huron ports have breakfast on the steamer, after which, on Wednesday and Friday mornings, the steamers City of Alpena or City of Mackinac are found nearly ready to sail. Mondays and Saturdays they do not leave until night, which gives an excellent opportunity to view the beauties of Detroit.

A trip of thirty hours by the City of Mackinac Wednesday mornings at 9 o'clock, and Saturday nights at 10 o'clock, or the City of Alpena Monday nights at 10 o'clock, and Friday mornings at 9 o'clock brings you to the great historic summer resort and sanitarium, Mackinac Island. At the hour of departure from Detroit our steamer springs on the stern line, and swings out towards the middle of the river, clear of all obstructions, and in a moment is

9

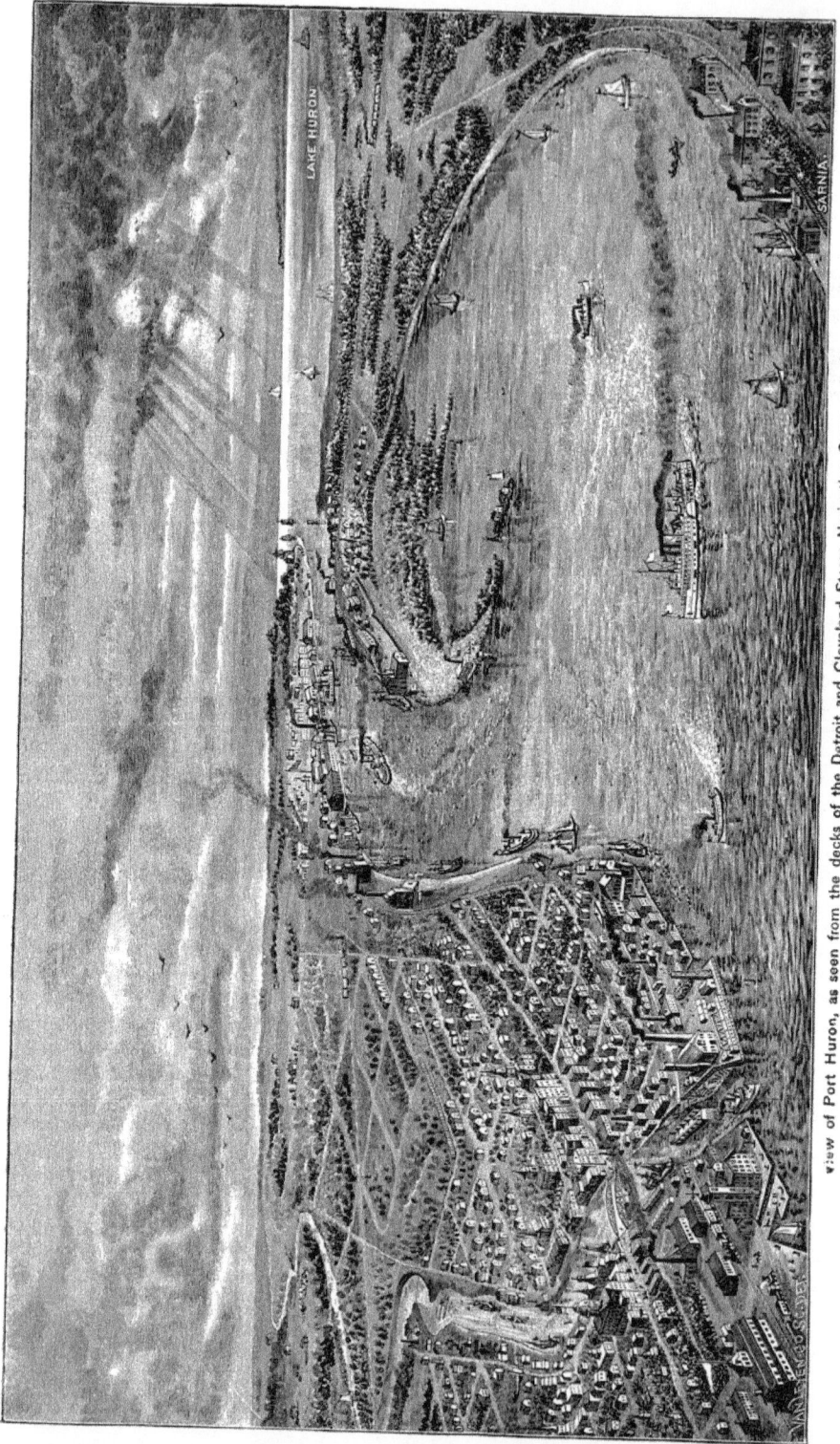

View of Port Huron, as seen from the decks of the Detroit and Cleveland Steam Navigation Company's Steamers.

PORT HURON, on the St. Clair river, at the foot of Lake Huron, is 62 miles from Detroit, and has 12,000 inhabitants. The soil is sandy, and consequently free from malaria, which, with water clear as crystal, and the cool breeze from Lake Huron, afford two great vitalizing elements of nature, pure air and water, making it a healthful city, and a pleasant place in which to pass a hot summer. On the opposite bank of the river (Canada) Sarnia, with 5,000 inhabitants, is beautifully situated, and has long been a great resort for Southern people. There are hotels and all conveniences for tourists. One mile above is Sarnia Bay, a paradise for sportsmen. Splendid fishing is found here, pickerel, bass and perch. Ducks of all kinds are shot in large quantities. At Fort Gratiot, one mile above Port Huron, the Grand Trunk R. R. Company have built two very large car building and locomotive shops. The fort established in 1814 was discontinued in 1879. Two miles north of Fort Gratiot is Huronia Beach, a famous resort for families, which is established on economical principles. At this point the lake narrows to the entrance of St. Clair river, and a fine view is had of the shipping. Often fifty sail of vessels, steamers and tugs are in view at once, presenting a panorama that is greatly admired. This resort, nestled among trees, consists of a long line of cottages, with a central dining hall. A white sand beach lies between them and the lake. The buildings are all of a neat style of architecture, and present an attractive appearance. Fresh water bathing is unsurpassed. Everything is made attractive, especially for children. Servants are not allowed to accept fees of any kind.

---

under full speed. Taking the channel on the east or Canadian side of Belle Isle Park, our course lies straight across Lake St. Clair, which is 22 miles long and 22 wide, to the St. Clair Flats. The entrance to St. Clair river through the narrow winding channels at this point was formerly attended with great danger. To improve and shorten the entrance, the U. S. Government constructed a ship canal, which was completed in 1871, at a cost of $653,550. It is 8,200 feet long, 200 feet wide, and 16 feet deep.

The St. Clair Flats belong to the government, and those who have built cottages, hotels and club houses, hold possession by the right of Squatter Sovereignty only. The buildings are set on dry land, made with earth dredged from around each site. Before many years the bank on the American side will be lined with public and private resorts. The St. Clair river is 48 miles long, 1¼ wide, and is the connecting link between the great upper and lower lakes, the water of which will pass over Niagara Falls and down the St. Lawrence river a few weeks hence. Unlike the great Mississippi, the beautiful Hudson, and other famous rivers, the waters of the St. Clair are always clear. Not only does the traffic upon this river impress one with the vastness of the commerce of the great lakes, but its continually changing panoramic views produce a lasting effect on the mind. A pen description can scarcely do justice to this magnificent stream, which possesses a magnetic attraction that of itself draws pleasure and health seekers to its shores.

It is the finest and purest stream of water in the world, the pride of the people who reside on its banks, and the admiration of tourists. These steamers stop on the river at Marine City and St. Clair on the up trip only. Port Huron is an important distributing point for the company's business to and from upper ports and points in the interior of Canada and Michigan. From Port Huron to the lake the river narrows, and the large volume of water poured into Lake Erie, causes a strong, rapid current. Passengers who are destined for Goderich and the Manitoba Country leave us here and cross the river to take the Sarnia line of steamers. The steamers do not stop at Fort Gratiot, as passengers who have come from Montreal and other points in Canada are taken by the Grand Trunk railway to Port Huron only a mile below. The steamers City of Mackinac and City of Alpena leave Port Huron

View of Sand Beach, as seen from the decks of the Detroit and Cleveland Steam Navigation Company's Steamers.

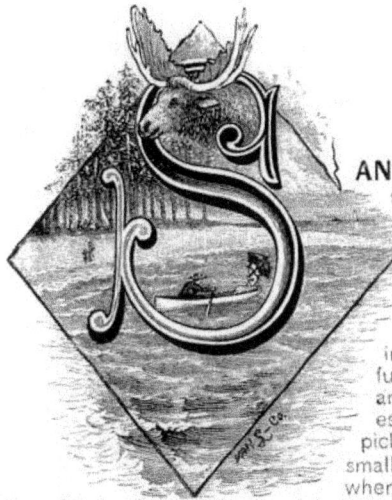

AND BEACH, 124 miles from Detroit, has a population of 1,300. A beach of fine, white sand slopes gently back to a natural terrace, which rises 30 feet. Back of this is a second terrace, 10 feet high, on which most of the village is built, commanding a fine view of the lake. Its harbor is formed by a breakwater 8,000 feet long, which cost over $1,000,000. It encloses 460 acres of still water, in which can float a large amount of shipping. This furnishes excellent opportunities for boating, fishing and bathing. A government life saving station is established here. White fish, trout, bass, perch, pickerel, herring, etc., are abundant. Angling for the small fry affords capital sport, but it comes to business when white fish and trout are caught, and there are no finer fish in the world when taken fresh from the deep, blue waters of the lake. The healthful, bracing air of Lake Huron makes it a desirable place near which to spend the hot season. The great body of fresh water lying east so modifies the heat and cold, that the atmosphere shows a temperature of remarkable evenness and healthfulness. The country back of this place is the only known habitat of the elk in Michigan.

On a steamer the captain's popularity should not hinge on the entertainment of passengers to the sacrifice of that vigilance on which the speed and safety of his craft depends. As Poor Richard says, "Lost time is never found, and that which we call time enough proves little enough." To be successful he must be strong of nerve, fertile of resource, of temperate habits, and possessed of judgment and common sense. The hurricane deck should be kept clear for the free exercise of his abilities in navigating.

---

going north Wednesday and Friday evenings at 16.30 o'clock, and Tuesday and Sunday mornings at 7.00 o'clock.

There has been so much of interest to take the attention for the past six hours that the trip through the lake is a pleasant relief. From this out all points of interest are seen on the port side, the Canadian shore being far away. We get outside, and from "abreast" of Fort Gratiot light the steamer is put on her course for 3¼ hours, which brings us to within 5 miles of Sand Beach, when we "haul in" for the harbor of refuge. The captain, who likes "lots of sea room," keeps well out into the lake. These large, iron steamers are not obliged to conform to the old adage, "Small boats must keep near the shore."

A short stay at this port, and our steamer resumes her course. Five minutes takes us outside the breakwater, and we head for Point Au Barques light, which is reached in one hour. This point is at the entrance to Saginaw Bay, which is crossed in two and one-half hours, a distance of 45 miles. This is the only stretch where land is lost sight of.

After passing this light, two trails of black smoke may be observed on the horizon. It comes from a sister steamer, which is due to pass at this half-way place. Officers and passengers are interested, and as the steamers pass, exchange a salute of whistles, shouts and waving of handkerchiefs. It is only for an instant, both are running at high speed, and are soon far apart. Our steamer's speed has brought into view the distant smoke of another steamer, going our way; she left Detroit twelve or fourteen hours ahead of us. We are fast overhauling her, and passengers become interested as they notice that great clouds of black smoke are thrown out more frequently from her one smoke-stack, in the vain effort to keep away from us. The fact is, the Detroit and Cleveland Steam Navigation Company's steamers are expected to pass everything they meet without extra effort.

"See! we are gaining on her!" "Yes, we will pass her within fifteen minutes."

"How fast are we going?" "Sixteen or seventeen miles an hour."

"How fast are they?" "Ten or twelve miles an hour. Some are not over eight."

"Do they carry passengers?" "A few. They run into small ports that this line doesn't touch, and because it was thought, naturally, that leaving twelve hours earlier, they

Bird's Eye View of Au Sable and Oscoda from the decks of Detroit and Cleveland Steam Navigation Company's Steamers.

SCODA, 180 miles from Detroit, has 2,000 inhabitants, and is located at the mouth and on the north side of the Au Sable river. The adjacent country comprises extensive forests of pine, and lumbering is one of its chief interests. It also has extensive salt works. The Detroit, Bay City and Alpena R. R. is completed to Alger Station, connecting with the Mackinac division of the Michigan Central R. R., making the inland towns between Bay City and Mackinac City easily accessible from this point. The town of Au Sable, located on the south side of the river, has a population of 2,500. As these ports have no harbor, piers are built from the shore reaching into deep water. "Eternal vigilance is the price of safety" is the motto of the Detroit and Cleveland Steam Navigation Company, and is thoroughly comprehended and seconded by their officers. The captain is clothed by the U. S. government with monarchial powers, and those who realize the importance of order and discipline to their comfort and safety will see much to admire in the thoughtful study and official watchfulness which makes this a thoroughly well organized system. When making a landing or leaving port, the captain on top of the pilot house, by turning a revolving cap can see the compass and direct the wheelsman, while by bell pulls and speaking tubes he reaches all parts of the steamer, and the Colossus obeys his will almost without a word. If not always in sight, he is not far away. In his room, immediately abaft of the pilot house, is a complete set of charts showing all the known shoals and dangerous points. A barometer indicates the weather, and a thermometer helps to conclude his calculations. If his eye is not on the binnacle in front, or the compass within the pilot house, a third compass stands near his desk, which is a tell-tale indicator of the watchfulness of mate and wheelsman left in charge.

would arrive at their destination as much in advance, but we will get through first, nevertheless, and this steamer on her return trip, will meet her again somewhere out in the lake, still working her way up slowly."

"Why, our steamer must get back to Detroit again a long way ahead!" "Oh, yes, she'll make two round trips while the other makes one. In the fall when the weather is rough, the steamers of this line run in and out of their ports about on time, leaving other steamers tied up to a wharf for favorable weather, while they are making one or two round trips."

"Then passengers miss it by taking any but this line?" "It makes no difference how anxious you are to get through, it's better to wait for the City of Mackinac or City of Alpena. You'll arrive at Mackinac Island ahead, every time, and even at Alpena as soon. When the Detroit and Cleveland Steam Navigation Company first established their line to Mackinac three years ago, with their elegant steamer City of Alpena (then called City of Cleveland) it was regarded as an experiment only, and short lived; the public were consequently slow in giving their hearty support to so much enterprise. The Company demonstrated their own confidence, however, by contracting for still another iron steamer of equal elegance, the City of Mackinac, which was put into commission the following season. These two beautiful steamers have now become household words, not only among the people along their route, but among the tourist public from distant parts, until their fame has reached all portions of our country and Canada, and the Company's methods and business principles have built up an important traffic in a wonderfully short time. But here we go past our friend, like an arrow shot from a bow, the craft soon becomes a mere speck, and our steamer is suddenly headed towards the shore for Oscoda. The arrivals of the steamers of this line are always an attraction for the people along the shore. Leaving the wharf again the steamer backs out for a quarter of a mile into the lake. The wheelsman throws his wheel over hard-a-port, and we run two miles straight out from the wharf in order to clear Miller's point, and a series of shoals extending from the main land, then throwing the wheel a-starboard, head for Harrisville. When directly opposite, she is headed at right angles from her course for the wharf. But

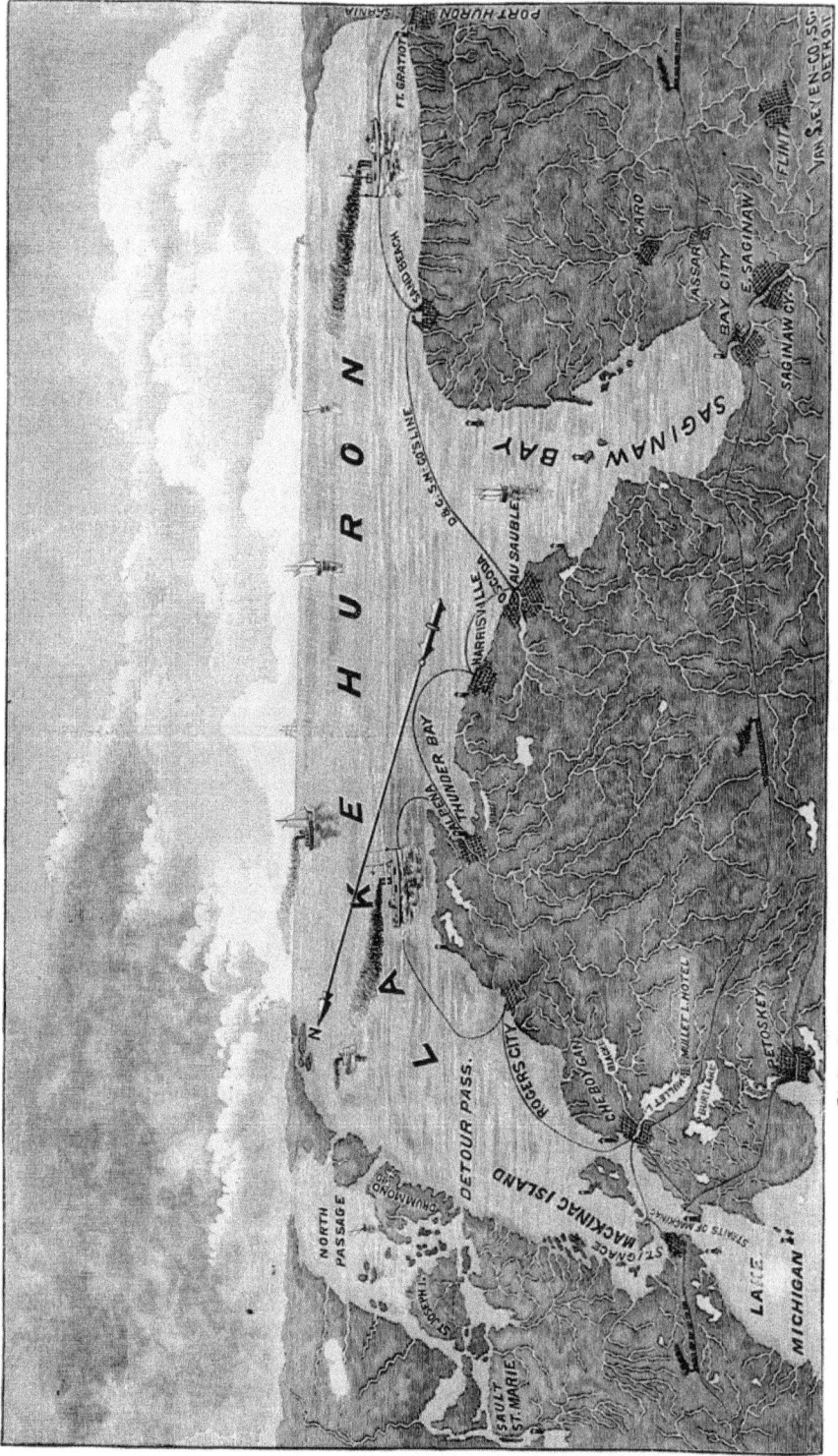

Bird's Eye View Lake Huron Division Detroit and Cleveland Steam Navigation Company.

hARRISVILLE is a flourishing village of 1,000 inhabitants, 197 miles from Detroit. The site is high, commanding a fine view of the lake, and justly claiming to be one of the many healthful locations of this wonderful northern Michigan. It has been visited by invalids with the most favorable results, and entertains hopes of some time being a favorite resort. Sixteen miles inland is Hubbard Lake, a beautiful sheet of water. Visitors find its scenery attractive, and in the abundance and variety of game it is the elysium of sportsmen. The lake is easily reached, and has been the favorite resort of many who have keenly relished the sport and reward for their efforts, in the game that abounds in the woods and waters of the county. Says a gentleman, a frequent passenger: " There is something characteristic about the Detroit and Cleveland Steam Navigation Company, a kind of individuality that to me is admirable, and the more I see of their thorough system, the more I am convinced that the officers on shore and on board are equally interested in a thoughtful study for the comfort of their patrons. It requires but little observation to realize that discipline and a strict attention to details are the key to the successful and quiet working of every department.

few lake ports have a harbor, and are obliged to build piers out into the open lake. Leaving the wharf again, we pass Sturgeon Point Light, then South Point, and when abreast of Thunder Bay river, shift the course a few points, and run into the river for Alpena.

How long will it take to reach the wharf? We can give no time as it depends altogether on the condition of things. The lumber kings may have been running logs down to their mills and choked it up, and some little time may be lost finding a tug to pull us in. While the city government clears up and improves the highways through town, their single, narrow highway of water is neglected, and the steam craft who serve them, unjustly suffer a heavy expense for tugs, broken wheels and loss of time.

There is a steamer close by us, she is lying still as though waiting for something. What does it mean? It is simply one of those cases where there is but little system used in the navigation of vessels, and although you can see by the moonlight that there is a broad expanse of water in the bay, still the safe channel is somewhat narrow, and unless steamers are careful to run in by a proper course, there is a chance of getting aground. Our friend is not sure of his bearings, and is waiting to follow us in, taking advantage of our courses. You may notice this lack of confidence frequently. Four officers are constantly watching the course of our steamer, and any variation would receive their prompt attention. This river is an important factor in the prosperity of Alpena. Approaching it by water the view is one which, though it may disappoint the searcher for the picturesque, means to the business man energy, bustling life, and commercial prosperity. The singing saws, rattling trucks, noisy mill engines, and numberless steam and sailing vessels passing in and out cannot but give to the practical observer the impression of a flourishing town; and indeed a happier combination of fertile resources and undaunted energy than is centered in this pleasant little city of the lakes would be hard to find. Lake captains say that during heavy fogs in the day time, the song of the saws, unlike the mythical siren lays that lured sailors to destruction, often helps them to find the entrance. While our steamer is discharging freight it will be interesting to take a stroll through the town, but keep watch of the whistle which is sounded for her departure.

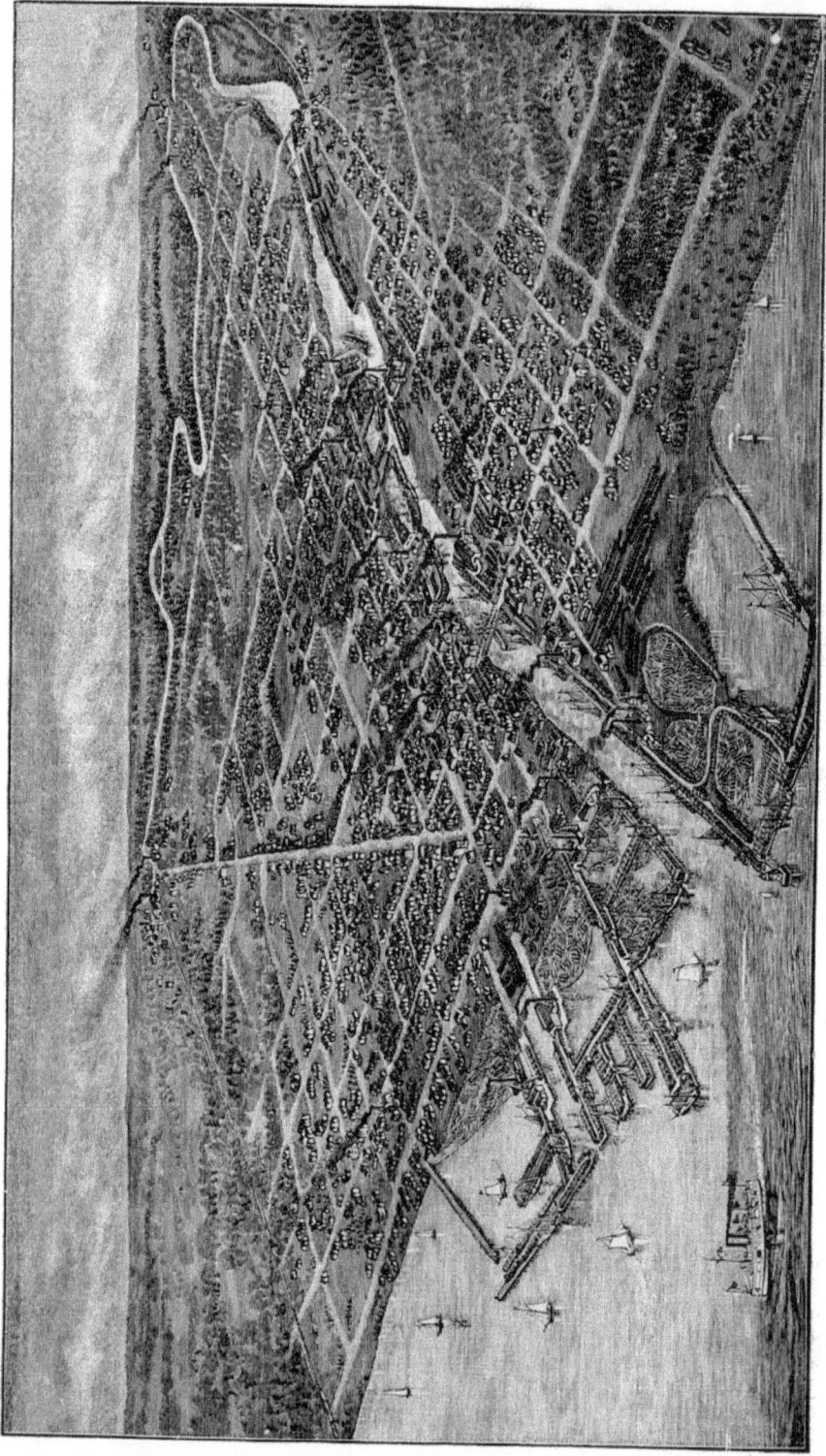

Bird's Eye View of Alpena, Mich.

LPENA is 228 miles from Detroit, population 10,500; situated on Thunder Bay, at the mouth of Thunder Bay river. It is the center of the lumber interests of the west shore. The wharves are constructed by driving piles on the water edge only, and filling with slabs, which are usually covered with earth. Some of the streets are made of sawdust. Lumbering commenced in 1858. Since then the advance has been rapid, and reflects credit on the energy, enterprise and ability which raised this city in a few years to the position of metropolis of the Lake Huron shore. Attention was first given to the fisheries in 1856. Nine tugs and twenty-five sail boats are now constantly employed in this enterprise. The principal grounds are at Sugar, Round and Sulphur Islands, Misery, Partridge, and North Points, and Ossinake. The regular fishing boats remain out during the season, which lasts until the water freezes, while the tug boats bring in each day's catch, returning with stores and provisions. From the U. S. fish hatchery thirty millions of young white fish were shipped in the spring of 1883, and planted in Thunder Bay, and Lakes Huron, Michigan and Superior. An important event of early days was the arrival of the mail, carried by Indians from Bay City to the Sault, following a course around the shore with a train drawn by dogs. The Iron City Club, of Pittsburg, camped, summer of '84 on Long lake, 7 miles distant. Their route was by rail to Cleveland, thence by the Detroit and Cleveland Steam Navigation Co.'s steamers.

Our company has been considerably reduced, and as preparations are going on for leaving port again, we find a new order of things. With care the steamer worked her way into the river, but it is another thing to get her out again. Between the floating logs and the crowded river, which is too narrow to admit of winding around, it becomes necessary to employ a tug, which takes our line and tows us out stern first, until clear of the piers, and room enough is found to handle the steamer. Our course lies well out into the lake, with the shore in sight all the way, and is a most interesting trip. On parting with the tug, our steamer keeps the shore aboard three miles away, giving the reefs of North Point, which extend two miles from land about the same distance. We round Thunder Bay Island Light as we come abreast of it, giving a wide berth to the shoals at the foot of the island, then come abreast of the light a second time, and resume our course northward. Many a craft has come to grief at this point, from over anxiety to get on her course. Life saving stations are located near this light, also at Middle Island and Forty Mile Point, in Hammond's Bay, at the north, and at Sturgeon Point, Ottawa Point, Port Austin and Point Aux Barques on the south.

Off our course, six miles to the north, when abreast of Middle Island, lies False Presque Isle, which has a fine lake. The bold, abrupt shore of Presque Isle admits of running close in, and affords a fine view. We make a short call at Rogers City. Spectacle Reef Light, seen in the distance, is most romantically located. Out by itself on a small flat rock, ten miles from shore, this light stands one hundred feet above the waters of the lake.

Suddenly the order comes "Starboard," and as the steamer's bow gradually turns towards the shore, Cheboygan river unexpectedly opens up to view, and we plow our way among lumber piles and floating logs, which so block the harbor at times that the services of another tug is required to take us in and out. Propellers, with their wheels less exposed, make things lively, and take out logs, boom and all into the lake. Here is an instance where it would seem that "might makes right," the pleasure of the lumber kings being more potent at Cheboygan than the local government, which they are largely instrumental in creating. Were a lot of farm wagons to block their street, the owners would soon be brought to account from these same obstructionists, but the shipping, the best element of

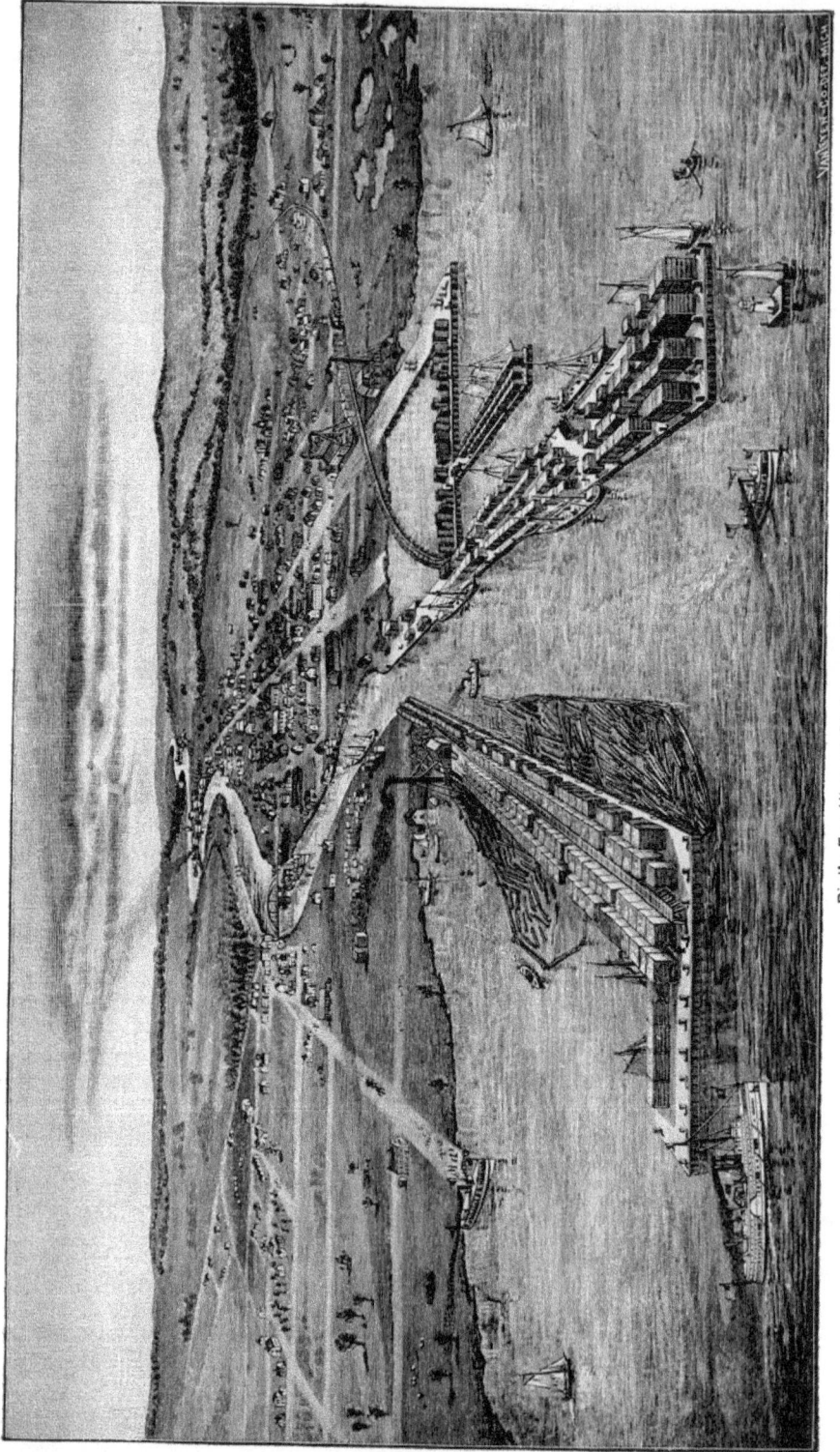

Bird's Eye View of Cheboygan, Mich.

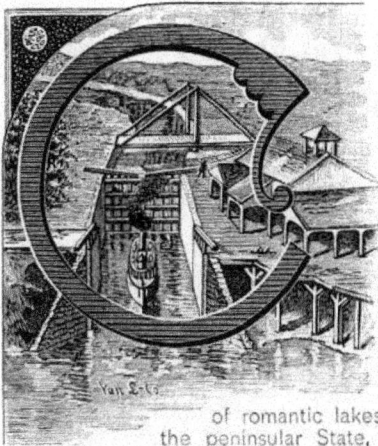

CHEBOYGAN, 329 miles from Detroit, and 16 from Mackinac Island, has a population of 2,000, and was settled in 1846. Situated at the mouth of the Cheboygan river, its location is one of the finest and most advantageous in the State. It has extensive lumber interests, and is the leading commercial city of the Straits. Among the natural advantages of the town are its flowing wells, which, being bored from twenty-five to seventy-five feet, throw the pure, cold water to a height of five feet, and even higher when tubed. Cheboygan river is navigable for small craft, and is the outlet of an extensive system of romantic lakes and rivers which cut across the northern part of the peninsular State, and connect the west shore of Lake Huron with the east shore of Lake Michigan, linking together Cheboygan, Petoskey, Harbor Springs, and the Traverse Bay region. A trip through this intricate inland route is a delightful novelty to the tourist, who is provided by the Inland Navigation Company with steamers which are constructed especially for the purpose, and which start from Mackinac Island. Arriving at Petoskey, should you prefer to return by another route, you can choose between the steamers on Lake Michigan or rail to Mackinac City, and thence by ferry steamer across the Straits of Mackinac to the island; the distance being forty miles. Michigan occupies a leading position in its attention to the culture and protection of fish. Doubtless this arises from the fact that the State is so largely surrounded by water, and has such an innumerable number of lakes and streams. One county, containing but 900 square miles of land has over 500 lakes which are clear bodies of spring water, with bold shores, some of which are beautiful beyond description. The intelligent and progressive fish commission of the State have annually planted the lakes and streams with millions of selected and hatched spawn.

---

their prosperity, must bear these indignities without redress. On arriving at the wharf, many passengers for Petoskey leave us and take the pleasant inland route through the crooked lakes and rivers. It is a novel trip, without it those who make their first visit to Mackinac fall short of a complete tour, and in connection with the Detroit and Cleveland Steam Navigation Company, it forms the only attractive and comfortable route from the east and south to this paradise for rest and recreation. Some make their first visit to Mackinac, and take the inland route from there, or go down by rail at their leisure.

As the whistle sounds the warning of departure, stragglers hasten on board, the gang plank is hauled in, and the steamer, tied to the wharf by a stern line, and laboring hard with the engine, slowly swings round in the narrow river, and works her way into the lake, or is towed out to the dummy light. Rounding this, we head for Mackinac Island, which looms up sixteen miles away. Its magnetic influence seems to be felt even at this distance. There is much to interest in this short run. A landscape of unrivaled beauty is spread out before us. On the port bow is seen Mackinac City, and farther on to the northwest looms up on the horizon the island of St. Helena.

The many trails of smoke in the distance are from steamers passing to and from Lake Michigan. Directly ahead are Rabbit's Back and the highlands of St. Ignace, at whose feet lies the town, apparently walled in by the Martel iron furnace on the left and ore docks on the right. On the starboard bow we see what seems to be one long, continuous stretch of shore, but which breaks away as we approach, and proves to be Bois Blanc, (Bob-low) Round and Mackinac Islands. In just fifty minutes from the Dummy, the captain is on a sharp look-out for the glimpse of Bois Blanc Light, (or its flash by night) which, being on the farther side of the island, can only be seen for a moment as we pass the intervening water to Round Island. On its reappearance on the other side of Round Island, the course is changed, and Mackinac Island and village are distinctly seen; another change, and the steamer, with a sudden turn swings quickly and gracefully into the crescent bay, upon whose shores once dwelt the red-skinned Ottawa, and about whose island home, rising three hundred feet above the clear, blue waters, still cluster the mystic halo of song, romance and legend.

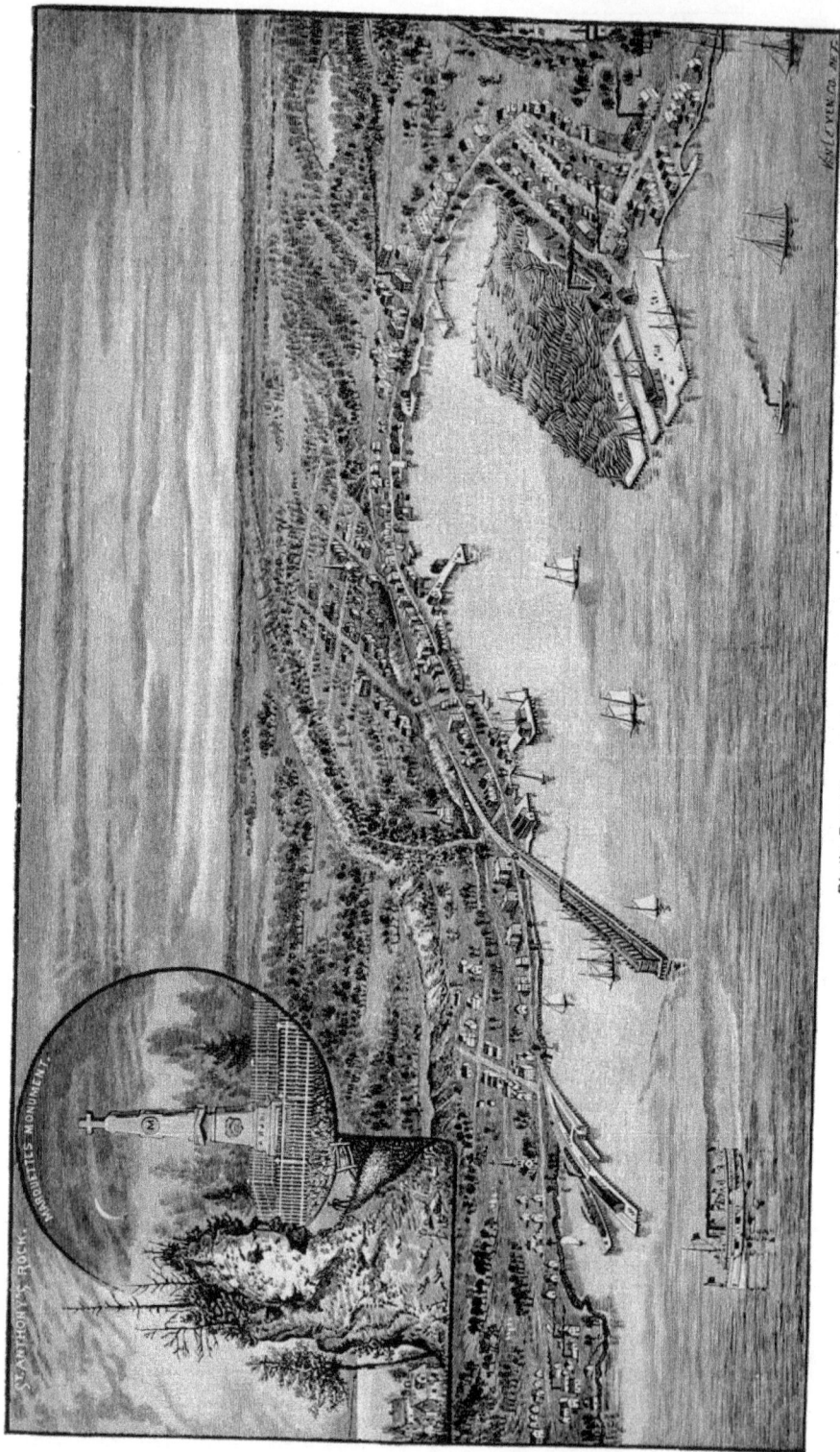

Bird's Eye View of St. Ignace, Mich.

T. IGNACE, 350 miles from Detroit, has a population of 3,000. The Gate City of the upper peninsula is singularly located; it extends in a semi-circle around the head of East Moran Bay for three and a half miles, and is almost wholly built on either side of one street. From forty to one hundred and fifty feet back from the lake, the land rises to a height of fifty feet, forming a terrace overlooking the vast expanse of water, and is most admirably and charmingly adapted for summer residences. The drive of four and one-half miles, to Groscap and along the winding shore to St. Martin's creek, embraces the water front of this young city; and St. Anthony's, Bear Face and Castle Rocks, Rabbit's Back and Lake Chechock, Marquette's Grave and the old Catholic Church are full of interest to tourists. St. Ignace was founded in 1671 by Father Marquette, and for a quarter of a century it was the center of interest in what was then the wilderness of Michigan. Near by clustered Indian villages, inhabited by six or seven thousand savages. It was from this place that Marquette set out May 17, 1673, in search of the Mississippi, then called the Great River. His bones were brought back four years later, and buried in a vault in the chapel which he constructed. After this chapel was burned his resting-place was lost sight of until a few years ago, when excavations brought to light fragments of the bark coffin and bones, which are carefully preserved as sacred relics. For a century and three quarters after the Jesuits becoming discouraged, burned their chapel, and returned to Quebec, the town ceased to be of any importance, all interest being centered on Mackinac Island. New life has recently been given it by the march of improvement, and it is now the shipping point for a large amount of ore, telegraph poles, ties, iron, and other products of the upper peninsula, it being the southern terminus of the Detroit, Mackinac & Marquette Railroad, which penetrates the upper peninsula as far as Marquette, on Lake Superior.

This Island Summer Resort is made famous from the magnificence of its scenery, its historic and military associations and Indian legends, while its grand and massive rocks, its smooth beaches of glittering sands, washed by the waves of the great unsalted seas, afford never-ending objects of interest. There are natural drives to many historic spots which teem with story of Indian and British warfare. Among the scenes of beauty and grandeur are Lover's Leap, Arch Rock, Sugar Loaf, Devil's Kitchen, etc.; and from the summit of the Island the eye rests with pleasure upon the fairest expanse of forest, fort, village and wave. Living streams of pure, cold water gush from the rocky precipices, and to those desiring grand scenery, pure air, abundance of simple, health-giving pleasures, and with mind refreshed and body invigorated, to return to the daily pursuits of business life, with pleasant recollections of a summer well spent, the Island of Mackinac pre-eminently offers special inducements. The great Straits of Mackinac, attractive in themselves are dotted with islands, and stretch their glittering waters into the dim distance. Many short excursions to other interesting spots help to make one's stay delightful. The longer and most attractive of these is up the Soo river to Sault Ste. Marie, on the morning steamers. By taking the Detroit and Cleveland Steam Navigation Company's steamers from Cleveland, Tuesday or Thursday evenings, and from Detroit Wednesday or Friday mornings, passengers for Sault Ste. Marie have the advantage of a daylight trip through river St. Clair to Port Huron the first day, also over the picturesque portion of the route from Alpena to Mackinac Island the second day, a shorter or longer visit to the island as desired, then a daylight trip up Soo river, leaving the island at a seasonable hour in the morning. This is a pleasant combination not afforded by any other line. There is much to interest at Sault Ste. Marie; old Fort Brady, the famous ship canal, and shooting the rapids in an Indian canoe are exciting experiences. Steamers of both American and Canadian lines pass through this canal en route to Lake Superior, which afford a choice of routes, via either the north or south shore.

Through Tickets at excursion rates can be obtained at principal railroad ticket offices.

Island of Mackinac.

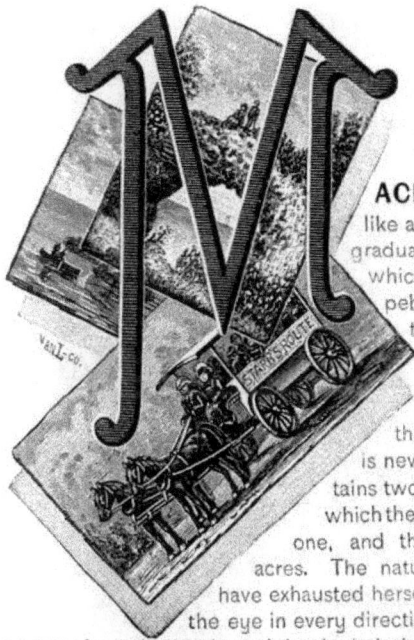

MACKINAC ISLAND, the rock girt, fairy isle, sitting like an emerald gem in the clear, pellucid wave, rises gradually and majestically from the crystal waters, which cover but cannot conceal the glistening, white pebbly depths beneath. It is the central point of the three great lakes. It knows no land breeze, hence the winds are always cool and refreshing, and seem incessantly tossing balls at each other. They no sooner cease blowing from Lake Michigan than they come from Lake Huron, and Lake Superior is never behind in the contest. Mackinac Island contains two thousand two hundred and twenty-one acres, of which the national park comprises eight hundred and twenty-one, and the military reservation one hundred and three acres. The natural scenery is unsurpassed. Nature seems to have exhausted herself in the manifold objects of interest which meet the eye in every direction. The lover of Mother Earth will hardly grow weary of wandering through its shaded glens, and climbing over its rugged rocks, each day bringing to light some new object of beauty and interest. Longfellow, in his poem of "Hiawatha" has put into English verse some of its wild Indian legends, which people every rock and glen with spectral habitants. Hiawatha is the Mena-bosho of the Algonquins, and the Island of Mackinac was considered his birthplace.

If the poetic muses are ever to have a new Parnassus in America, they should certainly fix on Mackinac Island. Hygeia, too, should place her temple here, for it is one of the purest, dryest, clearest and most healthful of atmospheres. The Island shows unmistakable evidence of the water having once been two hundred and fifty feet above its present line. It is a mooted question whether the lake has fallen from its original level, or the island has, from some cause, been lifted up. Springs of water, clear and cold, may be found at the base of the high cliffs, and scattered through other localities.

Mackinac village is a perfect curiosity in itself. Situated at the foot of the bluff, upon the brow of which stands the fort, it extends for a distance of a mile along the beach. The buildings are a mixture of the modern and antique, some of which were brought from Old Mackinaw when the town and fort were removed from that point after the massacre of June 4, 1763. Many of the fences are of the original palisade style.

Schoolcraft, who visited it in 1820, says: "Nothing can exceed the beauty of this island." It is a mass of calcareous rock, rising from the bed of Lake Huron, and reaching a height of more than three hundred feet above the water. Some of its cliffs shoot up perpendicularly, and tower in pinnacles like half ruined gothic steeples. It is cavernous in some places, and in these caverns the ancient Indians were wont to place their dead. Portions of the beach are level, and well adapted to landing from boats. The harbor at the south end is a little gem. In it, vessels can anchor and be sure of a holding, and around it, the little old fashioned French town nestles in primitive style, while above frowns the fort, its white walls gleaming in the sun. The whole area of the island is one labyrinth of curious glens and valleys. Old fields appear in spots which were formerly cultivated by Indians. In some of them are circles of gathered stones, as if the Druids themselves had dwelt there. The soil, though rough, is fertile. The Island was formerly covered with a dense growth of rock maple, oak, iron wood, etc., and there are still parts of this ancient forest left, but all the southern limits exhibit a young growth. There are walks and winding paths of the most romantic character among its hills and precipices. From the eminences overlooking the lake can be seen magnificent views of almost illimitable extent.

Mackinac Village, as seen from the Gun Platform of the Fort.

The late Dr. Drake says: "The island is the last, and, of the whole, the most important summer resort to which we can direct the attention of the infirm or the fashionable. The living streams of pure water, cooled down to the temperature of 44°, gush from the lime rock precipices, and an atmosphere never sultry or malarious, supersedes all necessity for nauseating iron, sulphur and epsom salts. As a health resort it is unsurpassed. Its cool air and pure water are just what are needed to bring back the glow of health to the faded cheek, and send the warm currents of life dancing through the system with youthful vigor." Its natural beauties and historic associations, together with the innumerable lesser attractions which cluster round about, serve to furnish visitors with so much entertainment and variety for either the robust or weakly ones, that ennui which eventually is felt at most resorts need not be experienced here. In Mackinac you eat with a new relish, and sleep like a child. You row, or ramble, scarcely able to keep your buoyancy within bounds. Dr. Mills, once post surgeon at Mackinac, says: "No better place can be found for sickly girls and puny boys, for worn out men and women, whether from overworked brain or muscle, or for those inclined to hypochondria. A change from the tiresome sameness of home scenes cannot fail to benefit all. From the hour of entering Lake Huron, your feelings will indicate that you have passed beyond the reign of miasma, fever, dyspepsia, blue devils and duns, and you look back upon the whole of them with gay indifference, or a feeling of good-natured contempt, as every turn of the steamer's wheel carries you farther into the temperate and genial climate of the lakes, and away from your perplexities. Under these influences real diseases may abate, and the imaginary ones be forgotten. In the celebrated white fish (classical name, coregonus albus, signifying food of the nymphs), is found a native whose acquaintance is liable to but one objection, that of destroying the taste for any other fish, and which, with the trout and potatoes of the island render all foreign delicacies superfluous. We would caution the gourmand, however, against an excessive use of trout, which are said to produce drowsiness, for those who visit Mackinac should be wide awake, lest some scene of interest should pass unobserved.

Besides the agreeable change of climate on reaching Mackinac, there is the new sensation to one who has not before enjoyed the novelty of an insular life, of having found an island retreat. To his jaded sensibilities all around him is fresh, a feeling of security comes over him, and when, from the rocky battlements of the fort, he looks down on the surrounding waters, they seem a bulwark of defense against the host of annoyances from which he has sought a refuge. Thus the curative state of mind begins to act on the body from the first moment, and this salutary mental excitement will not soon die away, for the historic associations, not less than the surrounding scenery, are well fitted to maintain it, and to make the invalid forget his ailments. Dr. Mann says, "A few whiffs of the air would make your lungs give a hygienic laugh. This air must have been left clear out of Eden, and did not get cursed. Children are crazy with animal spirits, and eat in such a way as to demonstrate the paradox that the quantity contained may be greater than the container." These extracts will no doubt meet with a hearty response from thousands who have visited Mackinac.

At watering-places generally, all the features of the surrounding scenery are soon familiarized to the eye, which then merely wanders over the commingled throngs of coquettes, dandies, dancers and idlers, and soon returns to inspect the real or fancied infirmities of its possessor. A visit to Mackinac reverses all this. The attractions of the surrounding region are of a different and more wholesome kind, and draw to them those who seek health and recreation, and offer a delightful hot weather asylum to all who need to escape from crowded cities or a sultry climate. Besides this, the voyage imparts a pleasing excitement to the faculty of observation, curiosity is stirred up to the highest pitch, and pleasantly gratified by the hourly unfolding of fresh scenes of nature, some new blending of land and water, a group of islands different from the last, or a shifting series of painted clouds seen in the kaleidoscope of heaven afford constant variety, while the frequent trips of the Detroit and Cleveland Steam Navigation Company's steamers enable you to return as soon as desired.

Constance Fennimore Woolson knew the charm of the place when she made it the scene of so many romances, among them being the novel "Anne," and the short sketches, "Flower of the Snows," "The Old Agency," "Jeannette," and "Fairy Island." *

Planks Grand Hotel, Island of Mackinac.

WHILE MACKINAC ISLAND is undoubtedly the most interesting and attractive of Northern resorts, it has always been lacking in that great necessity of modern summer retreats, sufficient hotel accommodations. This season, however, marks a most welcome change. The magnificent structure erected during the past winter at a cost of $250,000, is the finest summer hostelry on the great lakes, a worthy peer of the spot on which it stands. It has been christened "The Grand," and will be thrown open to the public on July 1st, under the auspices of Mr. John O. Plank, a name in itself a sufficient guarantee for the fulfillment of every promise. Studious consideration of all the most modern conveniences, as well as the hundreds of details contributing to the comfort, safety or pleasure of the guests, and utter disregard of the item of expense, has drawn within this charmed circle the perfection of science and art, as applied to the building and conducting of a modern resort hotel.

"The Grand" is located on a bluff at the western end of the Island, 200 feet above the lake, and facing the Straits of Mackinac. It is 650 feet in length, and four stories in height, surmounted by a pitched roof with dormer windows. Its architecture is of the "old Colonial" style, the distinctive feature being a colonnaded portico, upon which the windows of every floor open. This portico or verandah is 22 to 28 feet in width, and extends the entire length of the house, a magnificent promenade. From its outer edge spring Doric columns, extending to the roof line, 38 feet above. The general outline of the building is broken in its central portion by a slight projection, which, commencing with a handsome porte-cochere and rising far above the roof, forms a tower from which an expansive and uninterrupted view in all directions can be obtained.

The main entrance opens into a large rotunda, from which branch the smoking and breakfast rooms, dining hall and ordinary. The reading, reception and drawing rooms are also close at hand. These are all furnished in the most luxurious manner, and are entirely devoid of the usual cold, dreary hotel effect. Their front windows command an excellent view of the Straits. Both the drawing room and dining hall are mammoth, brilliantly lighted apartments. The latter is capable of seating 600 people. It is perfectly ventilated, and its vaulted ceiling 27 feet overhead, and handsomely decorated windows on three sides give an unmistakable air of grandeur.

The culinary department, in some senses the heart of the house, is said to be the most perfect ever put in operation in a first-class hotel. It receives Mr. Plank's personal attention, and a better table-d'hote cannot be found.

The guest rooms are all large, light and well ventilated, and sufficient in number to accommodate 1,000 persons. Each suite of front rooms is provided with a private balcony. This novel but highly attractive feature is peculiar to "The Grand," and does away with the annoyance of a public balcony in front of rooms.

The hotel is lighted by gas and electricity, heated by steam, and provided with an elevator and electric call bells throughout. It is also equipped with barber shop, bath rooms, billiard hall, steam laundry and a first-class livery.

Its spacious lawn, smooth, pebbly beach and large park have received many additions to their natural beauties, and are very attractive. Superior carriage roads lead to the village half a mile below, or penetrate the interior of the Island.

An orchestra will discourse music during meal hours, and enliven the verandah and ball room in the evening.

The rates, except for parlors and rooms with bath, are $3.00 per day, with special arrangements by the week or month

o

Arch Rock, Mackinac Island.

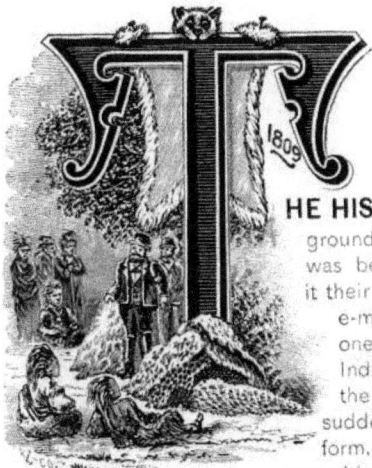

THE HISTORY OF MACKINAC, which renders it classic ground, may be divided into six periods. The first period was before the white man found it, when the Indians made it their rendezvous. Its original name is Me-che-no-mock-e-mong, given it as expressive of their surprise, when at one time at Point St. Ignace, a large gathering of Indians who were intently gazing at the rising sun, during the Great Manitou, or February moon, beheld the Island suddenly rise up from the water and assume its present form. From the point of observation it bore a fancied resemblance to the back of a huge turtle, hence the name.

The French called it Michilimackinac. Its present name Mackinac is pronounced Mack-i-naw. The Indians regarded this island with a species of veneration. Tradition credits it with being the birth-place of Michabou, the Indian god of waters, and the home of the giant spirits. It is said that in passing to and fro, the savages made offerings of tobacco and other articles to the Great Spirits in order to gain their good will. These deities were supposed to have a subterranean abode under the island, the entrance to which was near the base of the hill, just below the present southern gate of the fort. It was often the chosen home of the savage tribes, from the security which it afforded against their enemies.

The second period embraces the early voyages of Father Marquette, his founding of the college for the education of Indian youths, in 1671; the death of the explorer, and three years afterwards the remarkable funeral procession of canoes in which his Indian converts brought back his body from its first burial place on Lake Michigan, to the little mission on the straits of Mackinac, which in life he loved so well. The first pale faces who ventured into this region were Jesuit missionaries, who established the Ottawa mission at Sault St. Marie, the first permanent settlement in Michigan. The first vessel ever seen on these waters was the "Griffin," built by the explorer, La Salle, on Lake Erie in 1678. Thus commenced the third or commercial period.

The fourth or military period begins in 1695. At that date, Cadillac, who afterwards founded Detroit, established a small fort on the straits. Then came contests and skirmishes not unmingled with massacres, for the Indians enlisted on both sides. Finally the post of Mackinac, together with all the French strongholds on the lakes was surrendered to the English in September, 1761. The flags of three nations successively floated over this island. It has been the theatre of many a bloody tragedy. Powerful nations contended for its possession, and its internal peace was constantly broken by the white man's duplicity and the red man's treachery. In 1763 began the conspiracy of Pontiac, wonderful for the sagacity with which it was planned, and the vigor with which it was executed. Pontiac was the most remarkable Indian of all the lake tribes. He was a firm friend of the French, and to aid their cause, arranged a simultaneous attack upon all the English forts in the lake country. Among those taken by surprise and destroyed was the little post on the Straits of Mackinac at Old Mackinaw. A year afterwards, a treaty of peace having been made with the Indians, troops were again sent to raise the English flag over the fort. July 15, 1780, the British abandoned the fort at Old Mackinaw, and transferred the garrison to Mackinac Island, where they built the present Fort Mackinac. The history of modern Mackinac properly begins at this date. By a treaty of peace between Great Britain and the United States, signed September 3, 1783, the island fell within the boundary of the United States, but under various pretences the English refused to withdraw their troops. By a second treaty concluded November 19, 1794, it was stipulated that the British should withdraw on or before June 1, 1797. Two companies of U. S. troops arrived October, 1796, and took possession, a previous treaty with the Indians having secured from them the post, and the stars and stripes superseding

On the Beach at Mackinac Island.

the cross of St. George and the lilies of the Bourbons, waved for a time peacefully over the heights. During the war of 1812, the island was again surrendered to the British. After the victory of Commodore Perry on Lake Erie in 1813, an effort was made to recapture it, which proved unsuccessful. The troops sent were insufficient in numbers, the clumsy vessels which were to support them, could do nothing against the winds and waves, and not until the conclusion of peace in 1814 was the American flag again hoisted over the Gibraltar of the lakes.

The fifth, or fur trading period, opened in 1809, when John Jacob Astor organized the American Fur Company with a capital of two millions, and bought out the numerous struggling associations along the straits. For forty years this company monopolized the fur trade, and Mackinac, the great central market, was the busiest and gayest post on the lakes. These were Mackinac's palmy days. Her two little streets were crowded with people, and her warehouses filled with merchandise. Mr. Astor sold out in 1834. The energy and controlling influence which he had given the enterprise went with him; the company soon became involved, and in 1848 the business was abandoned. In its best days it was one of mammoth proportions. Here also the U. S. government made the annual Indian payments, when the neighboring tribes assembled by thousands to receive their stipend.

The sixth period is the summer resort of our modern times, which distinction is mainly owing to the facilities for reaching it recently afforded by three railroads and the steamers of the Detroit and Cleveland Steam Navigation Company, all of which center here, and for the want of which Mackinac, until within a few years, remained in a transition state.

The first steamboat to arrive at Mackinac was the Walk-in-the-water, in 1819.

Says a writer to the Congregationalist: "The trip from Detroit to Mackinac by one of the steamers of the D. and C. S. N. Co., was, I confess, a thorough surprise to me. The City of Alpena, in which we made our sail over this delightful route, is a large, splendidly equipped steamer. Great as is its speed, its motion is smooth and graceful as that of a swan. It is almost never either late or early."

Happily Disappointed.—Grandma's advice to lone females. An old lady from Cleveland relates her experience of a trip up the lakes, through the columns of the Leader.

"I may not be telling your readers anything new in relating some of the incidents of my trip to Mackinac, but there are too few Cleveland people who seem to have found out what an elegant place we have in this beautiful island to which we may flee for comfort and recreation. I must plead guilty to my own ignorance until unexpectedly, (for I had started Tuesday evening with the intention of going in a different direction), I found myself safely on board the steamer City of Detroit, together with two young lady friends, who had hardly recovered from the "set back" to our original plans. We had every attention from the officers of this magnificent steamer, and in the morning at 10 o'clock (Wednesday) we left Detroit, passing up the river with its beautiful scenery, across Lake St. Clair and through the canal into St. Clair river to Port Huron, where we launched out on the broad bosom of Lake Huron, and as there was nothing to be seen from the decks but unlimited green waters, on one hand, and a faint suggestion of land on the other, I gave some attention to the internal arrangements of the floating palace, on which it was our good fortune to find ourselves, and I have no apology to make for thus designating our good boat. It is no stretch of fancy, but a veritable fact, as your readers who have seen it will testify. There is nothing to be desired, or even remotely wished for, in the elegant appointments, and as regards the table, it is fully up to the standard of any first-class city hotel. As night comes on, we retire to the cozy state rooms; there is every inducement to enjoy a grateful rest and balmy sleep. Among my fellow voyagers were a party of over forty gentlemen and ladies, from Pittsburg, on a camping trip to Alpena, also a party of twenty or more young people from Bucyrus, O., intending to camp on the island. The grand old island is full of interest, but in our short stay only a hurried glance over the whole could be made. Our government has indeed chosen a lovely spot for a national park. Our three days' stay was soon over, and again the City of Mackinac steamed up to the dock, and we bade farewell to the island and soon found ourselves back in Cleveland. I hope that any lone females who may be at a loss where to go for a pleasant trip, will trust themselves to do likewise, and, in the care of Captain McKay and Steward Thorn, of the City of Mackinac, will derive as much pleasure as our little party, and in so doing, remember   GRANDMA."

OLD BATTLE-FIELD

Entrance to Fort Mackinac

Fort Mackinac, Mackinac Island.

FORT MACKINAC, built by the English over a hundred years ago, stands on a rocky eminence just above the town, and is now garrisoned by a small company of U. S. troops, and mounted by a few cannon of small calibre. There are various ways of reaching it from the village. Up the steps is probably the easiest, and the combined marine and landscape view from the gun platform is magnificent and well worth the effort to reach it. Below are seen the government stables, blacksmith's shop, granary and company's garden. On the battlements are the old block houses, pierced with port holes. Within the enclosure are the officer's quarters, guard house, barracks, commissary and magazine, with the hospital building just outside. When built, the fort was enclosed by a palisade of cedar pickets, ten feet high, intended as a defence against Indians. To make it impossible to scale this palisade, each picket was protected at the top by sharp iron prongs, and by hooks outside.

Starting from this spot, following the foot-path along the brow of the bluff overlooking the eastern part of the town, visitors fond of natural scenery will be delighted with the grand panorama of Nature which meets the view. Nearly three-fourths of a mile from the fort at the south-eastern angle of the island is the overhanging cliff, known as

Robinson's Folly. The legends connected with this cliff differ in the hands of different writers. One has it that "Captain Robinson, a great admirer of ladies, while strolling in the woods suddenly beheld a few rods before him a beautiful girl, who retreated as fast as he approached until finally she stood almost on the edge of the cliff, and in his eagerness to capture, as well as to save her from destruction should she lose her balance, the captain sprang forward to seize her, but just as he clutched her arm, she threw herself forward into the chasm, dragging her tormentor and would-be savior with her. His body alone was found. He was long mourned by his men and brother officers; but by and by it began to be whispered that the captain had indulged too freely in the fine old French brandy that the fur traders brought up from Montreal, and the lady was a mere ignis fatuus of his excited imagination, but the mantle of charity has been thrown over the tragedy, and a romantic explanation given in its place."

Another writer says: "After the removal of the fort to the island in 1780, Captain Robinson, who then commanded the post, had a summer house built upon the cliff, which soon became a frequent resort for himself and brother officers. Pipes, cigars and wine were called into requisition, for no entertainment was thought complete without them, and thus many an hour passed pleasantly away. After a few years, by the action of the elements, a portion of the cliff, together with the house, fell to the base of the rock, which disastrous event gave rise to the name." The brow of this cliff is 127 feet high.

Fairy Arch, or Giant's Causeway, lies a little to the north of this. It is an arch standing out boldly near the base of an immense rock, and is well worth the trouble of a visit. A walk along the brow of the bluff brings you to the far famed

Arch Rock. This is a curiosity which must be seen to be appreciated. Words cannot fully describe its grandeur. It is a magnificent natural arch, spanning a chasm of eighty feet or more in height, and forty feet in width. The opening underneath has been produced by the falling of great masses of rock, which are seen lying on the beach below. A path to the right leads to the brink of the arch, the summit of which is three feet wide and one hundred and forty-nine feet above the lake. From this dizzy height a most magnificent view presents itself. Below lies the broad expanse of Lake Huron, dotted in the distance with green gems

Fairy Arch, Mackinac Island.

of islands, and at the feet splashes its waves upon a pebbly beach, as if they were ever hastening to the bidding of Ariel's song: "Come unto these yellow sands." Descending through the great chasm we come upon a second area of less majestic proportions, but equally curious and wonderful, and looking up, the mighty arch seems suspended above us in mid-air. The rains and frosts have every year made great ravages, and the rock cannot long resist their action. Taking the road leading into the interior of the island, you soon reach

Sugar Loaf Rock. The plateau upon which it stands is about one hundred and fifty feet high, while the summit of the rock is two hundred and eighty-four feet above the lake, giving an elevation of one hundred and thirty-four feet to the rock itself. Its composition is the same as that of Arch Rock. Its shape is conical, and from its crevices grow a few vines and cedars. It is cavernous and somewhat crystalline, with its strata distorted in every direction. In the north side is an opening sufficient to admit several individuals. The view is very fine from the top. The curious are ever eager to know what freak of Nature placed this monstrous boulder in its isolated position, looking as though it had been thrust up through the earth like a needle through a garment. Traces of water action are seen on these two rocks, and are particular examples of denuding processes, which could only have operated while near the level of a large body of water like the great lake itself. To all fond of natural curiosities, these two rocks alone possess attractions sufficient to justify a visit to Mackinac Island.

Now, return to the fort and set out in another direction. Half a mile to the rear, and only a short distance to the right of the road leading to Early's farm is

Skull Rock, noted as the place in which Alexander Henry was secreted by the Chippewa chief, Wawatam, after the massacre of the British garrison at Old Mackinaw. Near the house now occupied by Mr. Early is that relic of 1812, the old Dousman house, across the road from which is the battle ground. A short distance down the road leading through this farm is

British Landing, where Captain Roberts disembarked his forces of English, French and Indians to take the island in 1812. The American troops, under Col. Croghan, also landed here in August 1814, under cover of the guns of the squadron, and marched to the edge of the clearing, (now Early's farm) where the enemy were in waiting. In a few seconds a fire was opened upon him, and the woods on every side literally swarmed with savages. After a vigorous attempt to drive the enemy from their stronghold, he was obliged to retreat with the loss of Major Holmes and several men. To the right of British Landing is a trail through the woods leading to

Scott's Cave, which is under one of the huge rocks peculiar to Mackinac. Its entrance is very low, but once inside a giant might stand erect. A most peculiar sensation comes over one on entering this dim cavern, and unless provided with a candle or lantern the visitor will find himself in almost total darkness. Strangers should not attempt the journey to the cave without a guide.

Leaving the town at its western extremity, and following the foot path around the brow of the high bluffs which bound the southwestern side of the island, or continuing along the beach close to the water's edge, for about a mile, you come to the

Devil's Kitchen, a cavernous rock, curious in its formation as well as its name. Near it is a spring of clear, cold water. A few yards farther on is the famous

Lover's Leap, a perpendicular bluff, rising to a height of one hundred and fifty to two hundred feet above the lake. The legend concerning it is that, long before the pale faces profaned this island home of the genii, Me-che-ne-mock-e-nung-o-qua, a young Ojibeway girl, often wandered there and gazed from its dizzy heights, to witness the receding canoes of the large war parties of the Ojibewas and Ottawas speeding south, seeking fame and scalps. Here she first met her lover, Ge-niw-e-gwon; here she sat, mused and sang her love songs, and here watched and listened for the return of the war parties, among whom she looked for her hero, whose head decorated with war eagle plumes, which none but a brave could wear, would be first turned to her. The wind often wafted far in advance the shouts of victory as they left Pe-quod-e-nong (Old Mackinaw) to cross to Fairy Island. Once when the party returned, she could not distinguish his familiar and loved war shout, and her spirit told her that he had gone to the happy hunting grounds. An enemy's arrow had pierced his breast, but ere he died he wished the mourning warriors to remember him to

FORT MACKINAC FROM THE OBSERVATORY AT FORT HOLMES

Fort Holmes, Mackinac Island.

the sweet maid. The girl's heart was broken, and she constantly saw her beloved beckoning her to follow him, appearing to her in human shape but invisible to others. One morning her body was found mangled at the foot of this bluff, her soul had gone to meet her warrior in the spirit land. Some distance from this is

Chimney Rock, which is said to be one of the most remarkable freaks of Nature. A foot path which leads from the beach near the base of Lover's Leap to the plateau above brings you to the Davenport farm, now owned by the Mackinac Island Summer Resort Association, where several elegant summer cottages have been built, and to which additions are made each season. A central building is used as a dining hall, from which meals are furnished at very near cost. Eighty acres have been neatly laid out and platted, and lots for the erection of cottages can be purchased on very advantageous terms. Last season's improvements aggregated over $20,000, one cottage costing $3,800. Having made the circuit of the island, let us ascend to

Fort Holmes, and seating ourselves look around from the high station built years ago by government engineers. We can see nearly every part of the island at our feet. The little clearings were once cultivated as gardens by American soldiers. Memory is busy with what has been written of scenes of the past as we gaze upon the adjacent islands, main land and the vast expanse of water surrounding us. Two hundred and fifty years ago, only bark canoes dotted its surface, then came the Canadian voyageur, rowing or paddling his large batteau, later the white sails of a sea-going vessel, and now steamers and vessels by hundreds rend the air with shrill whistles, or fling their white sails to the breeze, as burdened with the wealth of the nation and its precious lives, with swan-like grace and ease, they pass and repass like courtiers paying homage to their queen. Thus elevated above all that surrounds it, the panorama before us would justify the epithet to Mackinac of "Queen of the Isles." Up the Straits are green islets peeping above the waters, in front, Round Island forms a beautiful foreground, while Bois Blanc, with its light-house, stretch away to the east, and to the north are other islands which complete the archipelago. The mid-day beauties, however, vanish before those of the setting sun, when the boundless horizon seems girt by a fiery zone of clouds, and the brilliant display of skies paints itself upon the surface of the waters. Brief as they are beautiful, these evening glories quickly pass away, and the mantle of night warns us to depart while we may yet make our way along the narrow path.

Miss Woolson's writings have thrown a wierd witchery about Mackinac, and it has been to her a favorite spot for the locale of her romances. In answer to a letter asking for information, as to the number of times she had written of this place, Miss Woolson says: " I have often alluded to Mackinac in my sketches and stories. The second sketch I wrote (then beginning) was about Mackinac, it was called " Fairy Island," and was purely descriptive. There was, later, a short story of mine in the "Galaxy," called "Flower of the Snow," whose scene was Mackinac. But these were tentative merely. The first real description I gave of the island in print were two short stories, one called "The Old Agency," the other "Jeannette," both published in "Scribner's Magazines," now the "Century." Twice then, in my novel "Anne" the island appears again; it is the scene of the first quarter of that story."

Indeed, Mackinac might well be the scene of romances yet unwritten, not only on account of its unique and beautiful situation, but because of its native inhabitants, in whose strongly marked characteristics there is yet unmined material for the book-makers. Here are to be found people who were born on the island, have seen their three score and ten, and never yet stepped foot upon the mainland, those who taught the Indians in the old days of the mission, and the fashionable lounger of to-day. It is full of contrasts and surprises, and has long been called the "Wonderful Isle " from the fascination it seems to hold for all who have ever lived on its shores. One of the most enthusiastic admirers of the place whom we ever met, is an old gentleman now living in Chicago, who was a resident of Mackinac in the old mission days. Since that time he has seen the vast west grow from a wilderness to a mighty empire; he has seen Chicago spring from a smaller post than Mackinac now is, to the proud proportions of the western metropolis; he has been a potent factor in its growth, but he has never lost his affection for Mackinac, nor his desire to visit it often. He could not be persuaded to part with a portion of the land which he owns there, were it not to share the happiness of its possession with others. The Island is as important from a sanitary point of view, as it is attractive and beautiful from the aesthetic.

Devil's Kitchen.

Lover's Leap, Mackinac Island.

MARQUETTE, the metropolis of the Lake Superior country, nestles closely beside the broad bosom of the mighty inland sea. The high bluffs are crowned with handsome residences, which are surrounded by beautiful lawns facing on wide and well shaded streets. Its business section gives evidence of general prosperity, with stores bespeaking metropolitan tastes, and displaying all the requisites for comfortable and luxurious living. With the most salubrious climate, the purest of water, and the inspiration and refreshment of the pure atmosphere, it is only natural that it should be a rendezvous for tourists and health seekers. For those who love the rod and gun, it is most conveniently situated, being reached by the Detroit, Mackinac & Marquette Railroad from St. Ignace, on the Straits of Mackinac, at the terminus of the Detroit and Cleveland Steam Navigation Co.'s line of steamers from Cleveland, Detroit and Port Huron. The pilgrim destined for its hospitable environments, 150 miles distant, traverses the upper peninsula of Michigan, very properly designated and fast becoming known as a natural game reserve, selecting as he goes the choice spots to which he will return, armed with rod and landing net, or a more warlike equipment, certain in either case of obtaining ample reward for his efforts.

Notes from my Scrap Book.—" 'A straight trip to the Strait, where I pined for more pine,' wrote the man of the 'Hoosier,' forced to retreat from the merciless rays of a hoosier sun, which cooked his brain and dulled his faculties. He thanked his lucky stars that he came via Detroit, that he was permitted such comfort as was afforded by the City of Mackinac. No dust, no noise, no rattle or jar, no cramping seats, and no brakeman calling stations in unintelligible Greek; only a smooth, yet perceptible gliding onward of a huge floating palace; his delight was unbounded. He finally solved the Mackinac resort problem, as did his hoosier friends who read the front page of his well written sheets. Another scribe from Hoosierdom, he of the 'Wasp,' followed closely with his head lines very black and well displayed and his piracy on Mackinac had its desired effect: 'MACK-IN-AWE, or the Wasp man talks a little about MACK- and how he came to be IN-AWE.' His talk was, about Mack's big reputation, Mack's historical scenes, the wonderful events which had taken place on Mack. His pen pictures of panoramic scenes were vivid, for illustrations he referred to 'Picturesque Mackinac,' and finally, becoming weary of so much sight seeing, retired to the cabins, and fell to studying the characteristics of others. He found the usual variety viz: the real or pretended family of wealth, who held themselves aloof and managed to have things a little better than others. There was the old man whose love for travel and feminine society had not yet abated; the commercial man, the solidest man on board, dreadful flow of spirits, led conversation, told great yarns, knew more * * luggage? reduced to the vanishing point, eat? tells people 'its a cold day when he gets left,' violates all laws, last to retire, never ill, he was there. So was the young man, hail-fellow-well-met, among the roughs on the lower deck, maintained his standing with the aristocracy in the cabin, great favorite, clothes for every occasion, chums with a fellow equipped as if going to a lawn tennis party, who talks in a loud and familiar way about the ins and outs of water travel, etc.

52.LB. MASCALONGE.

CAUGHT AT THE CHENEAUX. BY ALF.DURPHY. SEASON 1886.

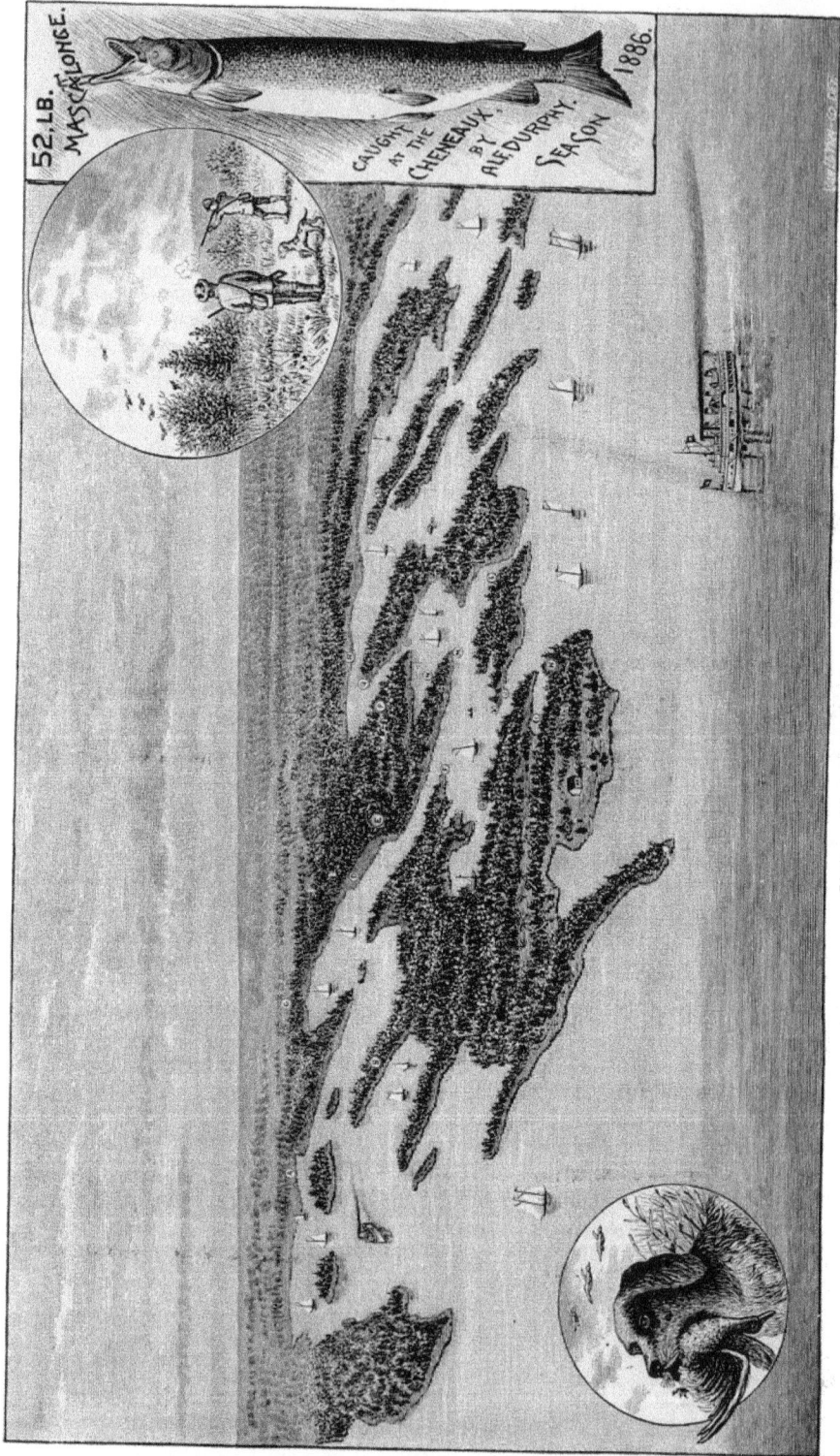

Birdseye View of Les Cheneaux Islands.

Les Cheneaux Islands (The Snows), one hundred or more in number, lie nestled together in a novel and attractive group near the north shore of Lake Huron, about fourteen miles from Mackinac Island, from whence they can be reached at any time by steamer or sail-boat. They are of all shapes and forms, two of the group, Marquette and La Salle, being of considerable size, while the others vary from one acre to mere fairy dots upon the water.

The picturesque beauty of this archipelago well repays a visit, while the trip thereto is one of the most delightful in the northern region and is the first to be taken by the tourist or resorter after doing Mackinac Island. The route for a time runs diagonally with the eastern shore of Mackinac, and a splendid seaward view of Robinson's Folly, Arch Rock, Fairy Arch and Giant's Staircase is thus obtained. As the distance increases, however, these bold cliffs sink within the outline of the Island, which in turn gives way to a distant view of the main land on the north. The surface of the lake hereabouts is dotted with innumerable small craft, a sunny sky of brilliant hue hangs overhead, and the oxygen laden breeze proves most exhilarating. The enchanted passenger forgets his goal, and loses himself in a congenial day dream, from which he is only awakened by the proximity of the shore, which has been approached unnoticed. A small channel is at hand, and the steamer, plunging into it, proceeds to pick her way through the labyrinth of islands and bayous which extends eastward for ten miles, the abrupt and curious windings exciting both awe and curiosity.

This network of narrow channels, with their deep pools and shady nooks, forms a splendid rendezvous for the finny tribe, and is undoubtedly the best fishing ground in the country. Bass, perch, muskalonge, Mackinac trout, pickerel and pike, of the largest and most gamey varieties, fairly swarm in all directions, and the most blase angler will find sport worthy of his mettle. Trout may be caught in the streams on the adjacent mainland, and the huntsman will find plenty of deer and bear, also small game.

Parties not intending to camp, should stop at Patrick's, which is situated nearly in the center of the islands. This hotel accommodates one hundred guests, and will furnish meals to campers, if desired, also boats, bait and guides.

Les Cheneaux Islands have, during the past three years, been the camp grounds of many important clubs, all of which sing loudly the praises of this veritable Sportsman's Paradise.

Below are particulars of the most advantageous points, as culled by our fisherman last season. The key shows their precise location on the birdseye view. Wood is plentiful everywhere. Hay can be obtained from Patrick's, and lumber from Hayne's mill.

A—Deep basin, with high, rocky shores. Best black bass fishery in the State—during east winds. **B**—Small clearing, with vacant cabin. High banks and good landing on north side. Bass, perch, muskalonge and some Mackinac trout. Near trout stream. **C**—Good trout stream. Reached by small boats from other points. Not easily found. **D**—Grassy bluff with good landing. Splendid camp ground. Large yellow perch, pickerel and pike. Five rods west, rocky bottom, home of the gamey black bass. Just south, home of Indian queen, over 100 years old. **E**—Patrick's Hotel situated on an elevation, back of landing, and adjoining a large camp ground. Black bass, rock bass, pickerel and perch. **F to K**—Deep, rocky bottom. Black bass abundant. **G**—Wisner's Sloping banks. Good camp grounds and landing. Empty cabin and open shed. Muskalonge Bay lies just west. Here muskalonge, pike and black bass may be caught, also large, red finned yellow perch, which are as gamey as the bass. Muskalonge weighing 28 pounds dressed, have been caught. Frogs abundant on lake shore of Island. **H**—Deserted cabin in clearing. Deep water, and good beach. Pickerel caught here have weighed 15 pounds. Large bass. **I**—Close Bay. Chickens, butter and eggs may be purchased here. **J**—Good camping spot. The finest pickerel fishing in America along this coast. Forty large pickerel may easily be caught in a day. At the point toward G, black bass and yellow perch. **L**—At mouth of third entrance and up channel. Black bass, rock bass and large sunfish. **M**—Rocky bottom. Black bass fishing. No landing. **N**—Ten rods from this shore is the ground of the large muskalonge. Heavy lines, gaff hooks, and skillful fishing necessary to land the fish. **O**—Rock bass and large sunfish. No camping place. **P**—Clearing, with cabin. Pike and pickerel on opposite side of channel. **Q**—Good camp ground. Bottom rocky. Black bass and large red-finned yellow perch. **R**—Haynes' dock and saw mill. Good black bass fishing. **S**—Sheltered bay in island. Deep rocky bottom. Black bass abundant.

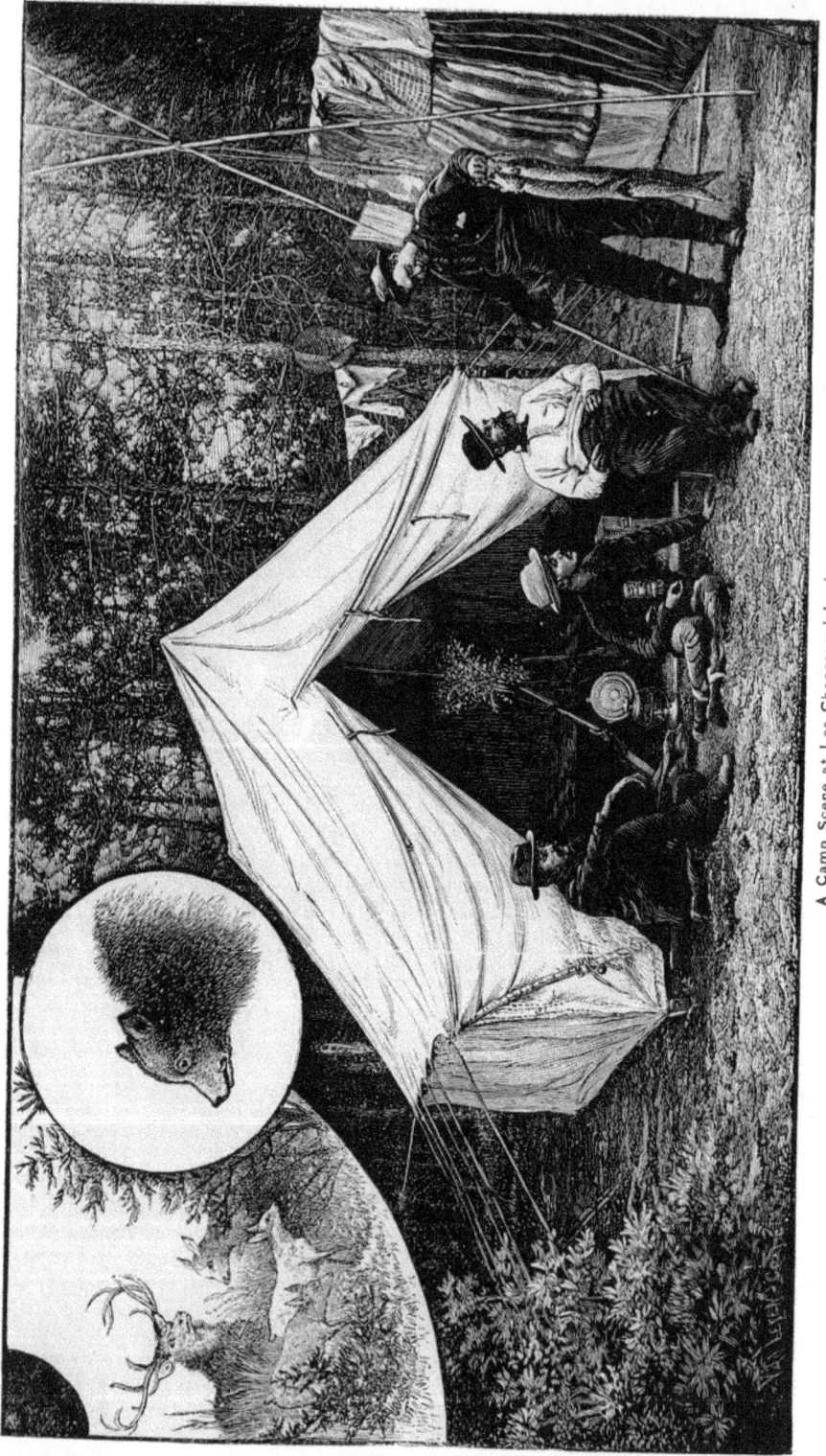

A Camp Scene at Les Cheneaux Islands.

ETOSKEY. In 1787, Nee-i-too-shing, "Early Dawn," a chief of the Chippewas, with others of his tribe, went down the lake shore on a hunting and trapping expedition, and camped on the Manistee river, at a point where the city of Manistee now stands. On returning to his rude home in the early morning, he put back the deer skin door and turned to look at the sun, which, as it rose above the horizon, flashed its first bright shafts of light into his lodge. At that moment the first cry of his new-born child came to his ear, and he exclaimed: "Neyas Pe-to-se-ga,"—Rising Sun. It was very fitting that the heir of "Early Dawn" should be thus titled. The home of this chief was seven miles northwest of Harbor Springs, and the time was when 4,000 warriors could be mustered from the regions about this bay.

At 22 years of age, Pe-to-se-ga took for a wife a maiden named Keway-ka-ba-wi-kwa, raised a family of fourteen children and became a chief and proprietor of nearly all the land now covered by the village site. Missionaries persuaded him that Neyas was an abbreviation of Ignatius, and thus he became Ignatius Pe-to-se-ga. The present village of Petoskey is indebted to this chieftain, who still resides within her limits, for her name, corrupted, Russianized or Yankeeized from the more musical and ancestral original. She certainly had no reason to be ashamed of her pedigree, for the chief for whom she was christened has many sterling traits of character. The old gentleman may be found at his comfortable home, a neat two story frame house on the bluff just beyond Bear River, on the outskirts of the town. He cannot be understood, however, except through an interpreter.

Petoskey is a charming summer resort situated on the south side and near the head of Little Traverse Bay at the foot of high bluffs. A more romantic location could scarcely be imagined. Little Traverse Bay is nine miles long; from a width of six miles at the mouth, the shores gradually approach each other until only two miles apart, forming the head of the bay into a half circle. The bay is here enclosed by high table lands or higher hills that approach the water in a succession of natural terraces, having the appearance of a vast amphitheatre, rising two hundred feet above the bay. In the center of this stands Petoskey, at an elevation of fifty feet. From this point the ground rises gradually to the natural limits of the town, thus giving to its denizens the benefits of the mild and invigorating breezes, and opening to all the beautiful views of the lake, bay and opposite shore.

The climate of Petoskey is a sovereign one for bilious diseases, hay fever, etc. The Western Hay Fever Association has its headquarters here. No watering place or summer resort on the continent can boast of purer air, fresher breezes, or better whitefish than Petoskey. The facilities for recreation are also good. The woods abound with game, and the rivers and lakes are full of fish. Bear river, which enters into Little Traverse Bay, near Petoskey, is a wonderful stream. Bear lake, its source, is twelve miles long and one mile wide, and is one hundred feet above the level of the bay.

If we are out in a boat on the bay and look in toward the land, we perceive that Petoskey occupies a series of picturesque undulations that spread out on either hand, and rise to the rear in the form of an amphitheatre. A lofty limestone cliff flanks the town on the west. Its top is crowned with trees, among which are discovered the tents of many vacation tourists who are "camping out." Behind them rises an overtopping eminence, dotted with pretentious villas of wealthy residents. From the verge of this cliff the outlook is superb. Across, five miles distant, is the ridge of hills that line the opposite side of the Little Traverse Bay. These sweep round in a symmetrical curve to the head of the bay two miles to the right,

Map Straits of Mackinac.

Bird's Eye View of the famous Mackinac Region, showing the Water Routes to Petoskey, Sault Ste. Marie and Lake Superior, and the D , M . & M R R to Marquette and Lake Superior. Good Fishing and Hunting

and then follow the hither shore until they rise and terminate in high cliffs. All along in that direction, as far as sight can reach, can be traced the white line of a pebbly shore limned against the green of the hills; and then, from the base of the cliff in a sweep of two miles or more to the left it forms a crescent, ending in a wooded point. Tree-covered hills slope gently back and upward from the beach, and pretty cottages peep out from among their branches. The principal part of the town lies in the bowl of the amphitheatre, from which a practicable road leads through a ravine to the long pier which projects from the hollow of the crescent into the bay. This pier gives additional character and life to the scenery.

Petoskey has a water front of 1½ miles, and extends inland about the same distance. It is of comparatively recent date. The locomotive engine, that vanguard of civilization, first pierced this almost interminable northern wilderness in 1874. It was not until just before midnight of the last day of that year that the first through train of cars reached the site where Petoskey now stands. At that time the surrounding country was a wilderness, but a few years have wrought a wonderful transformation. The village now numbers over 2,500 souls, and is rapidly assuming city airs. It is surrounded by a thriving and populous farming community. The transition from brush heaps, stumps and log houses, to graded streets, broad walks, fine stores and dwellings, schools and churches, palatial hotels, and a system of water works which a metropolitan city might well be proud of, has been magical.

Bay View, not quite two miles distant, extends one and one-fourth miles along the beach, and one-half mile back. It is a resort owned by the Michigan Camp Ground Association. It is the Ocean Grove and Martha's Vineyard of the north combined in one. Bay View is very emphatically Methodistic in its origin, history and purposes. A company of Michigan Methodists a few years since made a thorough examination of a large number of places, with a view of locating a State camp ground and summer residence, and finally decided upon this location as the most desirable. An association was formed, to which were donated 500 acres of land, on condition that a given amount of money should be expended in the way of improvements within a stated time. The relation has proved to be very fortunate, and the two-fold purpose had in view is being fully realized. Though but a few years have passed since the location of the grounds, Bay View has already become immensely popular. Large numbers from the east and south annually avail themselves of the privileges it affords, and the association is increasing every year.

It is beautifully located. The land rises from the bay in natural terraces, which afford delightful sites for residences. A great part of the land is platted into lots, and a large number of cottages, ranging in cost from $200 to $1,000 have been built. The Bay View cottages are supplied with clear, cold water through pipes from a never-failing spring on a hill side, seventy feet above the grounds. The cozy and picturesque residences built along the terraces facing the beautiful little bay, form most attractive and quiet summer homes.

Many points combine to make Bay View one of the most attractive summer resorts in the northwest. The bay itself is a gem of beauty, the grounds are delightful, the air is pure, the climate is healthful, the forests are grand, the water is excellent and the place is easy of access. There are a depot and wharf on the grounds with daily boats and trains. The society is good. Rents and other expenses are low.

A Word to the Wise.—There are thousands of people in the eastern and southern States who desire, during warm weather to flee from a hot to a cool climate, but unfortunately do not know whither to direct their steps. The sea-shore, fashionable watering-places, and the mountainous portions of the country are visited by some, and often without other satisfaction than a relaxation from business cares. An eminent writer, in comparing different sections of Europe and America, says that Nature has done more to render the country about the great lakes cool and healthful than any other portion of the globe. The Mackinac region with its outlying attractions, forms a fit setting to its sparkling island gem, which rests so gracefully on the great waters of this favored section. Knowing where to go, however, is but half the knowledge wanted, the next want is how to go, and how to enjoy the most en route. The best mode is to go direct to Cleveland, Detroit or Port Huron, and embark on the Detroit and Cleveland Steam Navigation Company's steamers, which afford elegance and comfort for all. Their common sense plan of furnishing berths and meals aside from the passage money, leaves the traveler free to economise or live in luxury, at will.   *

GITCHE MANITOU

VAN LEYEN-CO. Sc DETROIT

Giant's Staircase, Mackinac Island.

BOYD, OR "AUNT MARGARET," as she is familiarly called, is a woman with a history. She is an Ottawa Indian, born at Little Traverse over 70 years ago, and is a daughter of a right royal line of chiefs, as is evinced by the carriage of her head, the flash of her eye, and the beauty and smallness of her hands and feet. She has a fair education, and speaks English perfectly, has unbounded influence over the Indians, and has done important work in translating for the church, its books into the Ottawa language. Her sympathies are entirely with her people, she is humiliated at their degradation, and indignant at the wrongs they suffer at the white man's hands. In 1876, Margaret had an interview with the President in the interest of some Indian families who failed to receive from the government, deeds for their land. She was received with courtesy and assured that everything should be made right. President Grant, stumbling badly over her long Indian name, introduced her to his wife and several other ladies. Strangers always visit the antiquated Catholic church at Harbor Springs, founded more than two hundred years ago by Marquette. If the attendant priest happens to be absent, Aunt Margaret may generally be found at her house near by. She will unlock the church door, give a history of the mission, and recite the weird Indian legends of this lovely harbor.

Harbor Springs is on the north side of Little Traverse Bay, four miles from Petoskey and Bay View. The village is located on a beautiful harbor, formed by Harbor Point, projecting into the bay, and enclosing a surface of water a mile in length and half a mile in width. The Indians call this small bay Wequetonsing. The shore is a pebbly beach, washed by waters of such crystal purity that fish and other objects are plainly visible upon the bottom, at a depth of thirty to fifty feet. All along the waters' edge are large springs, from which gush streams of water as clear as air, and only twelve to fourteen degrees above freezing point, the health-giving properties of which are truly marvelous. The land rises some ten or fifteen feet, the business portion of the town being located on the level. Back of this rises an abrupt bluff seventy-five to one hundred feet. Fine building sites are found on the terraced plateau above. A small trout creek, starting from the springs, winds its way across the lower flat, and flows into the bay.

The history of the place is full of interest. Pieces of ancient pottery have been found here, indicating that it was once a stopping place frequented by the extinct race of mound builders on their journeys from Mexico to the Lake Superior mines. For ages it was a camping ground for the Indians, for whom it was well situated, its harbor being secure and abounding in fish. For many years it was a central point for the payment of annuities, and was a trading post next in importance to Mackinac. There are a few Indians still left who retain all the characteristics of their race. Among the many curious legends concerning the place, one relates to Devil's Pond, an innocent looking pool near the portage of Harbor Point, where the Indians believe the bad spirit dwelt until frightened away by the noise of the white man's saw mill. The scenery in this vicinity is beautiful: at the foot of the bluffs lies the picturesque village, then the harbor, a lovely sheet of water, reflecting on its placid bosom the drifting clouds, stars and trees, every tint being mirrored with perfect distinctness. Beyond is the open bay, with the surrounding shores rising in a succession of wooded hills. Through the trees on the opposite shore is seen Bay View and Petoskey, and to the right is the broad expanse of Lake Michigan. Eighteen miles west from Petoskey, on the shore of Lake Michigan is located the charming village of

Charlevoix, near which, between Round and Pine lakes, is the Chicago Summer Resort and the Charlevoix Summer Resort, comprising seventy-five acres.　　　　✳

Scott's Cave.

A Characteristic Drive, Mackinac Island.

AULT ST. MARIE, via Petoskey and Mackinac Island. One of the grandest trips in the world. How B. and W. spent a week. The beautiful steamer "City of Mackinac" left Detroit at 22 o'clock Saturday night, landing us in Cheboygan Monday morning, at 5 o'clock. A stroll through the town gave an appetite for breakfast, which we obtained at the hotel near by. The steamer "Mary" came in from Mackinac Island, and left the adjoining wharf, at 9 o'clock for a trip to Petoskey, by the wonderfully novel and attractive Inland Route, through crooked rivers and beautiful lakes. Our baggage was transferred to this landing without expense, and we boarded the little steamer, which headed up the Cheboygan, picking her way through logs, which generally obstruct the river. An industry peculiar to northern Michigan was indicated by busy sawmills; and though piles of lumber obstructed our view, we caught glimpses of our winding course, in time to save a dawning conviction that the trip must end there. A sharp angle brought to view a lock, the rear gate of which was closed. On our entering, the water from the river, ten feet above, was gradually let in from the bottom, and our craft lifted to the upper level.

Three miles above this point, Black river empties into the Cheboygan, and is the outlet of Black lake, which is twelve miles from the junction of the two rivers, and covers an area of six by four miles. Rapids, within a few miles of the lake, make further navigation by steamer impossible. A panorama of beautiful landscape is opened as we proceed, and Mullet lake, with its placid waters, wooded shores and attractive spots for camping was reached before noon. The lake is six miles above Cheboygan, and is a beautiful body of water, twelve miles long, and from five to eight wide. It is full of fish, and its borders abound in game. Into it empty Pigeon, Indian and Sturgeon rivers. On the right, nearly across the lake, is Topinabee. The Northern Hay Fever Association, Pike's Hotel, Railway station, telegraph office and stores are located here. Three miles farther on is the Mullet Lake House, where we stopped for dinner. This fine summer hotel, which is situated on a beautiful spot overlooking the lake, cost $50,000, has seventy-five large, airy rooms, elegantly furnished, and is especially attractive for families, being a paradise for children. The house opens June 20.

Soon after dinner, we proceeded by a smaller steamer, the "Northern Belle," which though drawing but thirty inches of water, often gets very near the bottom. At the bend in the river one could easily jump ashore from bow or stern. This species of miniature navigation presents many little surprises to the tourist, which serve to while away the hours and fill the mind with pleasant recollections.

Soon after leaving the Mullet Lake house, we entered Indian river, which some poet has likened to a "silver thread on Nature's carpet." Seven miles of beautiful river scenery, and Indian river village is reached, few of these crooked miles, which cover all points of the compass, would make only three as the crow flies. Fishing and shooting parties in boats, were met, and towed by our accommodating captain to points farther on. After leaving this romantic little village, we had fallen into a quiet contemplation of our novel surroundings, when we were startled out of our reveries by a shrill whistle, seemingly coming but a few feet away from the bank of the river, and the next moment we were hardly less surprised to see the small steam yacht "Louie" suddenly shoot out from behind a bend just ahead. It seemed a saucy affair, both the whistle and the sudden appearance; the little craft as much as saying: "Look out there! I claim the right of way here!" She contained a pleasure

Sugar Loaf Rock, Mackinac Island.

party, and the engineer, some eight years of age, sat unconcernedly by the boiler, answering signals given by the captain at the wheel. It seemed at times impossible to navigate so crooked a stream, the steamer going at the bank as if it meant to jump it, but a clever turn of the wheel brought us out all right, causing little damage—to the shore.

A conspicuous sign on the bank indicated that the cluster of Indian huts, settler's cabins and tents of tourists was styled "Columbus Landing," and while gazing at it, the steamer shot into Burt's lake, unnoticed. An odd looking steam craft seen off at a distance, proved to be a floating saw-mill, which ties up to the farmer's docks, and saws their lumber almost at their doors. At the small wharves along the shore, the steamer, if signalled, will stop. In case there is no landing, passengers frequently come out in small boats. Burt's lake is ten miles long and five wide. It is fed by Crooked, Maple and Sturgeon rivers, all large streams. Maple river is also the outlet of Douglass lake, which lies two miles north. Once across this lake we suddenly swung in apparently for the shore, but no; it proved to be for the mouth of a river, narrower and more crooked than we had yet seen. The passage of Crooked river, seven miles long, was the most highly interesting and novel portion of the trip. We wondered how the steamer would be able even to enter, as floating logs filled all the space, the very mouth being closed by a boom to keep them in. A rope was hitched to the stake, which the steamer pulled out, letting the boom go, and we went at the jam of logs at full speed, jumping some, pushing others with pike poles, and so making our way in amongst them. The river drivers, with red pantaloons and spiked boots, skipped around on the logs with a careless indifference to their uncertain footing, that would have sent a novice into the water at short notice. With their pike poles they rendered efficient aid, and after much pushing, pulling and butting, we finally got clear. Once more well into the river, our attention was absorbed with the navigating of the little steamer. Owing to the narrow, winding course, at times it seemed impossible to go farther, but by making very short turns and winding around abrupt angles, we threaded the labyrinth, being able, quite often, to pick evergreens from the shore on either side. Bump she would go into the bank, her stern swinging in, and off again for the opposite bank, and so on for miles. A short distance beyond the jam of logs, a lighter, containing kitchen and bunks, was being floated along, to be within easy reach for meals and shelter for the men on the drive just passed. Farther on was the tail end of the drive, a single man gathering stray logs into a raft, his boat tied astern. It was all very interesting, the scenery beautiful and the whole affair novel in the extreme. We shortly entered Crooked lake; which is five miles long, and famous for bass fishing, and numerous delightful locations for camping along its shores. In a few moments we were landed in the woods at Odin, at the head of the lake; and we bade good bye to the little steamer and its good natured captain with regret.

The Dummy, another novelty, was waiting at the station to take us the last eight miles of our journey, over the G. R. & I. R. R. track, to Petoskey. Its open cars afforded a splendid view en route, of the Bay View, Harbor Springs and Point resorts for cottagers. As we looked across the beautiful bay, the whole scene reminded us of an amphitheatre on a grand scale. Our train stopped at the Arlington hotel in time for supper, and a stroll about the young but famous town, before the departure of the train for Mackinac City, 33 miles away. We then took the ferry steamer "Algomah" for Mackinac Island, 7 miles distant. Some of our fellow passengers stopped at Mackinaw City over night, at the Wentworth house, which is over the railroad station, and went over to the Island in the morning.

While this is only Monday night, we have seen so much, and every moment has been so thoroughly full of enjoyment, it seems a week since we left our busy cares behind. A stay on Mackinac Island until Wednesday morning affords an opportunity of seeing the wonders of the place, so wisely reserved by the government as a national park, about which so much has been written, and to which so many pilgrimages are annually made, increasing steadily each year, as returning tourists tell of the sights seen, and the invigorating influences of the delightful trip.

On this trip, however, our time being short, we hunted up the "charioteer" before retiring, and engaged a seat in the chariot for a morning ride over the "Star Route," which comprises the most wonderful of the many wonders to be found. Fifty cents was the charge for this ride of about 7 miles. Another trip is made in the afternoon, or one can take a carriage and go farther. A walk over the by-paths will also be interesting. Here, invalids,

*

LEANING ROCK

Robinson's Folly, Mackinac Island.

VAN LEVEN CO

who would hardly think of doing so at home, walk long distances in the bracing air without fatigue. One of the ferry steamers generally makes the trip to Hundred Islands (Le Cheneaux) for the day. This disposed of Tuesday, and the following morning, after breakfast, one of the day steamers called, on her way from Cheboygan, and we jumped aboard for a trip up the beautiful Soo river (Sault St. Marie) Skirting the rocky cliffs of the Isle, we passed down the west shore of Lake Huron. At noon a landing was made at Detour, just at the entrance to the land locked waters of the Soo, whose repeated changes from a narrow entrance to a broad lake, then to a narrow, rapid river, and again to lakes, rivers and rapids, and its crooked courses around islands, which the currents have thus far failed to wash away, form a varied and charming experience scarcely ever surpassed. The passage of the Soo river must be made by daylight, and vessels are timed accordingly. Should they arrive at night, they anchor until the early dawn. The steamers of this line are the only ones that make the passage by mid-day. The channels are narrow, shallow and crooked. Boulders and shoals hidden just out of sight, lie all about, and sailors keep a sharp look-out here. The Sault St. Marie river connects lakes Superior and Huron, is sixty-two miles in length, and forms the boundary between the United States and Canada. Its mouth is a mile wide. Drummond's Island lies on the east, the main shore of Michigan on the west of the entrance. Pipe Island is four miles; St. Joseph's Island, Canada, with its old fort, eight miles; Lime Island ten miles; and Round Island eleven miles from the entrance. Potagannissing Bay, dotted with numerous small islands lying to the eastward, communicates with the north channel. Mud lake, six miles farther on, is four miles in width. Sailor's Encampment Island is twenty miles from Lake Huron, and is a famous camping place. There is excellent fishing and shooting; and supplies, small boats and small steam craft can be readily obtained. Here are found families, parties and fishing and shooting clubs, who for a short period seek relief from the strain of business, social and domestic cares, and the stifling atmosphere of closely packed cities. With a simple outfit consisting of wall tent, rubber and woolen blankets, a few tin dishes, and a compliment of cast-off clothing, they leave their homes, offices and school-rooms, and come out to this delightful region, assume the free habits of the natives, eat, sleep and are merry as seldom before, gain health and strength from the first breath of the pure, dry air of this wonderful Mackinac region, and return to their various callings with renewed vigor and a new lease of life. Hay fever sufferers, who are wise, come before the appearance of the annual attack, and wholly escape the malady, while even the tardy ones find their sufferings at once mitigated.

Continuing our course, the steamer seems to be heading straight for the shore, until a narrow outlet comes suddenly into view, and we enter the Nebish Rapids, passing between Sailor's Encampment and St. Joseph's Islands. From this on is to be seen the most varied and charming scenery. Indian villages, settlements and beautiful farms, serve to make a most interesting panorama. Lake George, six miles farther on, is an expansion of the river, nine miles long and four wide. It has thirteen feet of water over the shoals, and terminates at Church's Landing. Squirrel Island, Canada, lies opposite. Garden River Settlement, three miles distant, is an Indian town in Canada. Little Lake George comes next, then Point Aux Pines. Three miles farther, we pass around the head of Sugar Island, and eight miles beyond reach Sault St. Marie, fifty-five miles from Lake Huron at six o'clock in the evening, having supper on the steamer. Sault St. Marie is fifteen miles from Lake Superior, and there is much that is interesting about the odd old place. Here is situated the famous ship canal, built by the State of Michigan for the purpose of passing the rapids. The U. S. Government enlarged this canal, and constructed a new ship lock 615 feet long and 80 feet wide, having a lift of 18 feet. The scene witnessed on passing through the canal locks, is most interesting and exciting. The ship canal, river, island, and the two villages are in sight on either side of the stream. The Indians in their birch canoes are engaged in taking white fish below the rapids

And ne'er till lost is mem'ry's power,
Shall we forget the thrilling hour
Of our swift passage down the "Soo,"
In "Indian John's" light birch canoe.

Fort Brady, erected in 1823 is an old and important U. S. military post. Contiguous to this Indian village, it commands the St. Mary's river and the ship canal.

Grand Saloon Steamer City of Cleveland.

In the vicinity of the Sault St. Marie are several streams where sportsmen go in search of speckled trout. The nearest points are the rapids on both sides of St. Mary's river, and the small streams between the islands on the Canadian side. There are also several places from one to five miles above and below the falls where anglers resort. Indians, or half breeds, with canoes, have to be employed as guides. Our evening was fully occupied inspecting the government works, which well repay a visit. The immense and perfect structure of masonry, the water power made to run all the machinery necessary to operate the monster gates of the lock, and the dynamos which furnish the electric lighting, were perfect in all details, and quite in keeping with these was the neat, tidy appearance of all the surroundings. The ingenuity of man is conspicuous in the easy manner with which this ponderous affair is manipulated. As all the shipping from the lower lakes passes through this canal, tourists for Lake Superior have a choice of numerous steamers of either the American lines, via the south shore, or the Canadian lines, via the north shore route. We witnessed the locking of the most considerable amount of tonnage which had ever passed through the canal at one time. It consisted of two of the largest steam barges, with two immense consorts. The advantages of taking the Detroit and Cleveland Steam Navigation Company's route to the Soo are: it takes the west shore of Lake Huron, the passage of the rivers by mid-day, and includes the attractions of Petoskey and Mackinac Island at the least expenditure of time and money. Leaving Cleveland Tuesday or Thursday evening, and rising at four, the first morning only, all the interesting features are seen by daylight.

Thursday morning, at 6 o'clock, we commenced our return trip, arriving at Mackinac at 16 o'clock, and in two hours our favorite City of Mackinac came in from the south again. We went on board for supper, while the steamer crossed to St. Ignace and back, and bidding the island a final adieu at 20.30 o'clock, arrived at Detroit Saturday morning at 1.10 o'clock. As we had until 22 o'clock that evening before the steamer left for Cleveland, where she would arrive early the following morning, we enjoyed the pleasure of showing the beauties of our own city to our fellow passengers from the southern terminus of the route.

An Enchanted Spot.—Says the well-known writer, Miss Alice E. Ives, in the Detroit Post, Aug. 11, 1884, "I never had much faith in the attractions of Mackinac. I supposed that people went there because it was the correct and fashionable thing to do, or because the guide books had deluded the public with highly colored descriptions, and that there was considerably more talk than cider about the whole thing. Consequently when I took the City of Mackinac for the round trip it was with the settled conviction not to remain more than a few hours. I was deaf to all entreaties to stay. I pleaded work which could not wait and a wardrobe which was all contained in a shawl strap. * * * 'It will well repay you,' urged a friend who had seen nearly all this country, and part of Europe, and I began to weaken. * * *

When the steamer ran up to the wharf and the familiar faces of many Detroiters nodded a pleasant welcome from below, I was far enough in the toils to feebly acquiesce in the proposal to see what could be done about accommodations. * * * The charm of the place had began to tell upon me. * * * We climbed to the top of the bluff, entered the citadel, and looked over the parapet on one of the grandest views of the world. The great blue lake seemed to lap the yellow sands with a soft caress, and to fold upon its bosom the far-away purple shores drowsing in the still air of the dying day. * * * It needed no Calypso to make the thraldom perfect. * * * I determined when I did go back it should be on the City of Mackinac. It was so clean, so pretty, so sweet even to daintiness, and so strong and staunch, the officers were so gentlemanly, and the discipline and attendance so perfect, I couldn't think of stepping foot on any other steamer. This meant a longer stay, but I didn't seem to mind that now, and when our friend embarked for the down trip, I regarded him with a sort of pity, as one who had turned his back upon paradise. * * * Quaint old legends haunt every wooded knoll, cave, bluff and romantic walk. The opportunities for strolling and exploring are legion, and when tired there is always the luring charm of the pebbly beach, and the great expanse of blue waters. The old settlers are fruitful subjects for study. * * * As we once more stood on the deck of the beautiful steamer City of Mackinac, a lady said: 'It seems as if we were only sailing away for a little while and that we must surely come back to it again, as if we could never quite leave the enchanted island.' Verily Mackinac is an enchanted island, and unlike the land of the lotus eaters, where it was always afternoon, it seems with its fresh, clear, invigorating air to be always morning." *

Detroit and Cleveland Steam Navigation Company's Steamer City of Alpena.—Forward Saloon.

Lake Erie Division—Going North—From Company's wharf, 23 River St., Cleveland, 15 min. is consumed in getting out of the river. From the end of the piers the course is W. x N. $\frac{1}{4}$ N., $3\frac{1}{2}$ hrs. Pt. Pelee Light, 50 miles; W. x N. 25 min., Pt. Pelee Island Light; W. $\frac{1}{4}$ N., 1 hr. 10 min. to Colchester Light Ship; 1 hr. to Bar Pt. Light Ship; round Bar Point and into the river by courses N. W. x N. $\frac{1}{4}$ N., 6 min.; N. x W. $\frac{1}{4}$ W., 5 min.; N. $\frac{3}{4}$ E. $4\frac{1}{2}$min.; N. x E. $\frac{3}{4}$ E., 11 min., to Bois Blanc Isl. Light; N. $\frac{1}{4}$ W., 4 min., to abreast of Amherstburg, Can.; N. x W. $\frac{1}{4}$ W. 3 min., head of Bois Blanc Isl.; N. x E., 5 min., Lime Kiln crossing; N. W. x N., $\frac{3}{4}$ N., 19 min., head of Grosse Isle; N. $\frac{3}{4}$ E., 5 min., Mammy Judy Light; N. $\frac{1}{2}$ W., 5 min., abreast of Wyandotte; N. $\frac{1}{2}$ E., 5 min., abreast of Grassy Isl. Lt.; N. $\frac{3}{4}$ W., 6 min., to a point on Fighting Isl.; N. E x N. $\frac{1}{4}$ N., 23 min., Sandwich Mineral Springs; N. E. $\frac{1}{2}$ N., 7 min., Sandwich Point; N. E. $\frac{1}{2}$ E., 8 min., M. C. R. R., Detroit.

Lake Huron Division—Going North—From Co's wharf, ft. Wayne st., Detroit, E. $\frac{1}{4}$ N, 23 min.; N. E. $\frac{1}{2}$ N., 10 min., Windmill Pt. Light; E. N. E., 13 min., Light Ship; N. E. $\frac{1}{2}$ N. 56 min., Gov't Canal, into St. Clair river, keeping the middle of the stream to Ft. Gratiot Light; N. $\frac{1}{4}$ W., $3\frac{1}{4}$ hrs., N. W. x N., 20 min., Sand Beach; N. E. x N. $\frac{1}{4}$ N. 8 min., N. N. W., 1 hr., Pt. Aux Barques Light; N. W., $2\frac{1}{4}$ hrs., W., 10 min., Oscoda; E. N. E., 8 min., Miller's Pt.; N. N. E., 1 hr. 10 min., W. x N. $\frac{1}{2}$ N., Harrisville; N E. x E, 12 min., N. N. E., 10 min., Sturgeon Pt. Light; N., 1 hr., South Pt.; N. W., $\frac{3}{4}$ N., 1 hr., Thunder Bay River; into the river to Alpena; S. E $\frac{3}{4}$ E., 40 min., North Point; E. N. E., 20 min., Thunder Bay Isl. Light; N. N. E., 5 min., Thunder Bay Isl. Light, second time; N. N. W., 1 hr., Middle Isl; N. W. x N., 55 min., Presque Isle Light; W. x N. 1 hr. 5 min., W.S.W.10 min., S. x E. 3 min., Rogers City; N. x E. $\frac{1}{4}$ E., 3 min.; N. x W. 12 min.; N. W. $\frac{1}{4}$ W. 1 hr. 42 min., Spectacle Reef Light; W. 40 min., Cheboygan Light; W.S.W., $4\frac{1}{4}$ min., Cheboygan river, into the river to Cheboygan; N. W. x N., 50 min.; N., 5 min., N. E. x E., 5 min., Mackinac; W. N. W., 25 min., St. Ignace.

Lake Huron Division—Going South—From St Ignace; E. S. E., 25 minutes, Mackinac; S., 7 min., range of Bois Blanc Island Light; S. E. x S., 53 min., Dummy Light; up the river to Cheboygan; N. E. x N. $\frac{1}{4}$ N., 6 min., Cheboygan Light; E., 30 min., Spectacle Reef Light; S. E. $\frac{1}{2}$ E. 1 hr. 30 min.; S.S.E. 20 min.; S. x E. 6 min. Rogers City; N. x E. $\frac{1}{2}$ E., 3 min.; E. N. E. 10 min.; E. x S., $\frac{1}{2}$ S., 1 hr. 5 min. Presque Isle Light, S. E. x S., 1 hour, Middle Island; S. S. E., 50 min., Thunder Bay Island Light; S. S. W., 6 min. Thunder Bay Island Light, second time; S. W. x W., 25 min. North Point; N. W. $\frac{1}{4}$ W., 40 min., into Thunder Bay River to Alpena; S. E. x S. $\frac{1}{2}$ S., 1 hour and 5 min., Black River; S. $\frac{1}{4}$ E., 40 min., Sturgeon Point Light; S. W. x S., 15 min., abreast of wharf, W. x S. $\frac{1}{4}$ S. 5 min., Harrisville; S. E., 8 min., S. $\frac{1}{4}$ E., 30 min., Miller's Point; S. x W. $\frac{1}{4}$ W., 20 min.; S. W. x S. 15 min., abreast of wharf; W. x S., 5 min., Oscoda; E., 3 min., to clear the river; S. E. $\frac{1}{4}$ E., 2 hours and 40 min. Point Aux Barques Light; S. S. E., 30 min., abreast of Port Hope; S. x E., 30 min., abreast of harbor of refuge; S. S. W., 8 min., Sand Beach; E. S. E. 8 min.; S. $\frac{1}{4}$ E., 3 hours and 50 min. abreast of St. Clair River; S. W. x S., $\frac{1}{2}$ S. 10 min. to Ft. Gratiot; into the river, keeping in the middle of the stream to Gov't Canal; S. W. $\frac{1}{4}$ S., 53 min., Light Ship; S. W. x W. $\frac{3}{4}$ W., 13 min., Wind Mill Point Light; S. W. $\frac{1}{4}$ S., 7 min., Belle Isle Light; S. W. x W. $\frac{1}{4}$ W., 12 min., Walkerville; S. W. x S., 13 min., abreast of Wayne street wharf, Detroit.

Lake Erie Division—Going South—From Mich. Cent. R. R. wharf, foot of Third st. Detroit; S. W. $\frac{3}{4}$ W., 4 min., Sandwich Point; S. W. x S. 5 min., Fort Wayne; S. W. x S. $\frac{3}{4}$ S., 16 min., Fighting Island; S. $\frac{1}{4}$ W., $3\frac{1}{2}$ min. Grassy Island Light; S. $\frac{1}{2}$ W., $8\frac{1}{4}$ min Mammy Judy Light; S. x W., $4\frac{1}{2}$ min.; Grosse Isle; S. x E., 16 min., Lime Kiln Crossing; S. x W. 3 min., head of Bois Blanc Island; S. $\frac{1}{2}$ E., 3 min., Amherstburg; S., $4\frac{1}{2}$ min., Bois Blanc Light; S. x W., $\frac{1}{2}$ W., 10 min., out of the river; S. $\frac{1}{4}$ W. 5 min., S. x E., 5 min.; S. E. $\frac{1}{4}$ S., 2 min., Bar Point Light Ship; S. E. x E. $\frac{3}{4}$ E., 55 min., Colchester Light Ship; S. E. x E. $\frac{1}{4}$ E., 1 hour and 5 min., Point Pelee Island Light; S. E. $\frac{1}{2}$ E., 25 min., Dummy; S. E. $\frac{1}{4}$ E., 3 hours and 25 min., Cleveland Piers; then into river, to wharf at Cleveland.

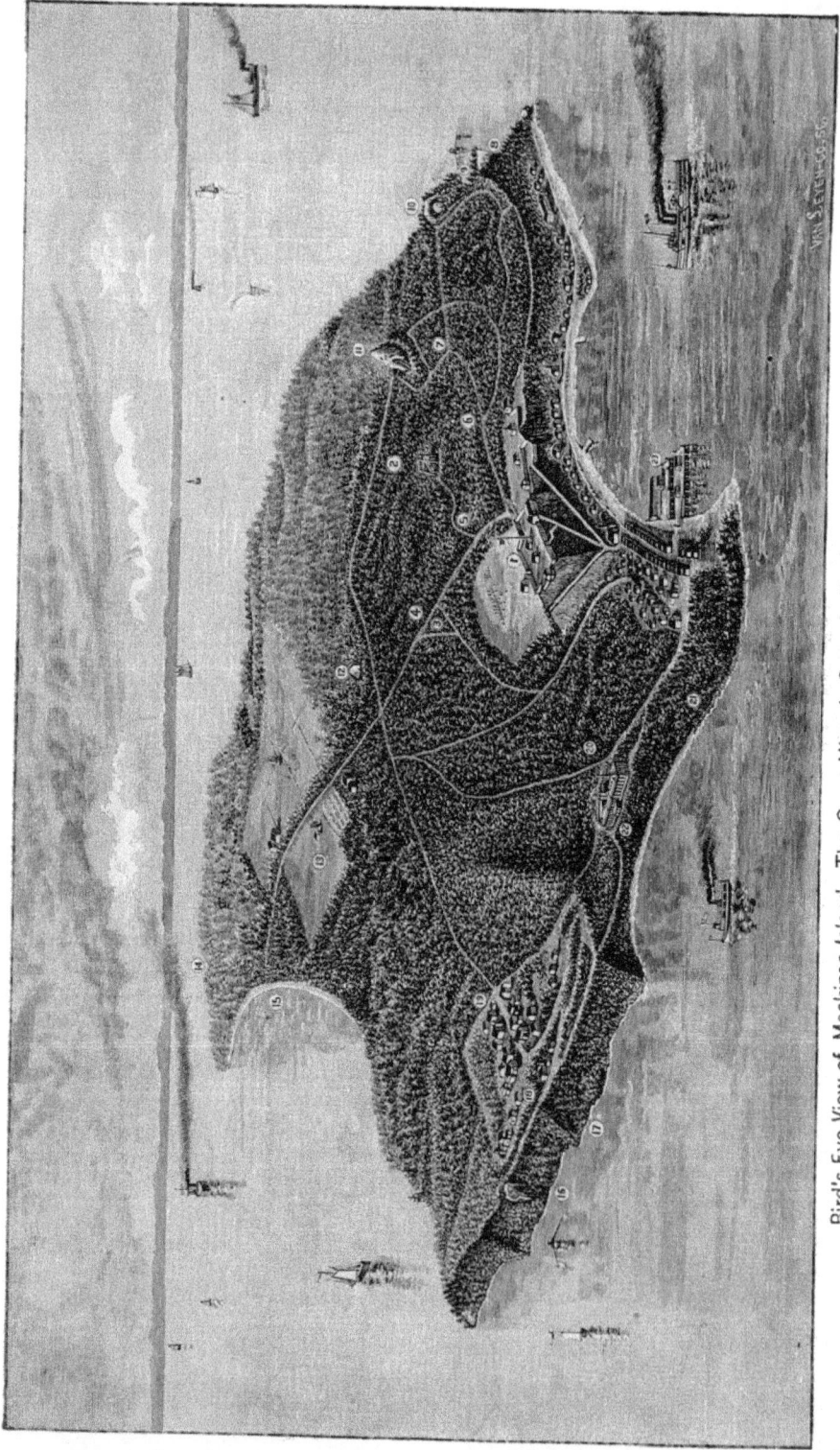

Bird's Eye View of Mackinac Island—The Great Historic Summer Resort and Sanitarium—National Park.

1. Fort Mackinac.
2. Fort Holmes.
3. Catholic Cemetery.
4. Military Cemetery.

5. Skull Cave.
6. Quarry, 1780.
7. Limekiln, 1780.
8. Robinson's Folly.

9. Cliffs.
10. Arch Rock.
11. Sugar Loaf.
12. Skull Rock.

13. Battlefield, 1814.
14. Scott's Cave.
15. British Landing.
16. Lover's Leap.

17. Devil's Kitchen.
18. Pontiac's Lookout.
19. Obelisk.
20. Old Indian Burying Ground.

21. Distillery, 1812.
22. Plank's Grand Hotel.
23. Det & Cle. Steam Nav. Co's Wharf.

www.ingramcontent.com/pod-product-compliance
Lightning Source LLC
Chambersburg PA
CBHW032030040426
42448CB00006B/791